NAVIGATE THE INVESTMENT JUNGLE

NAVIGATE THE INVESTMENT JUNGLE

Seven Common Financial Traps and How to Sidestep Them

DOUGLAS STONE

LIONCREST
PUBLISHING

NAVIGATE THE INVESTMENT JUNGLE

Seven Common Financial Traps and How to Sidestep Them

ISBN   978-1-5445-0831-3 *Hardcover*

      978-1-5445-0830-6 *Paperback*

      978-1-5445-0829-0 *Ebook*

This book is for Jennifer. Thank you so much for standing by me and encouraging me to tackle this project. Without your support and encouragement, this book might not exist.

It's also for Jeremy and Madison, both of whom have shown an interest in helping others navigate the investment jungle. I hope this book will play a role in guiding you both on the path of financial knowledge.

Finally, this book is for my clients, past, present, and future. You motivate me to keep learning and sharing my knowledge.

CONTENTS

Author's note: To protect the identities of people described in these pages, pseudonyms are used throughout.

INTRODUCTION

It was the year 2000. The tech bubble was growing fast and tech stocks were increasing rapidly in price—if not in value. The profits were out of this world. It was tempting to believe that they always would be.

Nonetheless, I was determined to stay grounded. As a registered investment advisor, I always seek to hedge against the downside of any investment. That's simple due diligence. With the prices of tech stocks exploding into the stratosphere, I was looking for a way to hedge against volatility. If they crashed, how would I protect my clients from the worst of the downside?

While I was pondering this question, I heard a sales pitch from some mutual fund wholesalers. I liked their pitch and accepted what they told me—that mutual funds were a good way to hedge against market volatility.

Based on the information they gave me, I bought my clients into a range of their products. I had bond funds. I had high yield bond funds. I had corporate bond funds. When the market went down, those funds should have gone up, right? That was why I had them. Unfortunately, that didn't happen. When the tech bubble burst, everything dropped through the floor at the same time. Something was wrong with my strategy.

A QUESTION OF RISK

As I reviewed my clients' accounts, I realized that the makeup of their portfolios wasn't working. They were exposed to too much market risk. My task as their financial advisor was to eliminate as much risk as possible, so the bursting of the tech bubble was a major wake-up call. One thing was clear: I needed a different approach, a new game plan.

The more I investigated my clients' portfolios, the more obvious it became that they all suffered from a similar flaw: as long as markets were doing well, they yielded high levels of profit. When the markets went down, however, these same portfolios were poorly set up to minimize losses. I had been told that mutual funds would perform this role, but reality firmly disabused me of that notion. When the tech wave crashed against the shore, mutual funds had done little or nothing to limit the damage.

At that point, I took a step back. I started questioning the products I was using and did my own thorough research. I educated myself on the true purpose of mutual funds and discovered that in many cases they serve the seller, not the investor. It was an eye-opening realization that has reshaped my whole perspective on financial planning.

Nowadays, when I see other advisors using mutual funds, I suspect they haven't done their due diligence. They know that if they add mutual funds to their clients' accounts, they receive a commission, and that alone convinces them it's the right thing to do. Often, it isn't.

Please don't think that I'm against advisors earning money. We work hard for our clients and we deserve to see solid profits. I firmly believe, however, that the financial success of an advisor should *never* come at the expense of a client's best interests. We should *always* ask whether a particular product helps our clients achieve their goals. If it doesn't, it's not a good choice.

The mutual fund representative I'd spoken to assured me that the funds had a great track record. In a market that had shown consistent growth for years, they probably did.

What the rep didn't mention was how the same funds performed when the market dropped. He was more interested in telling me how much I could earn when clients used the products. When the tech bubble burst, I found out for myself how they performed in a downturn.

I hold my hands up and admit that I, like most everyone else in my profession, drank the Kool-Aid. In the midst of the tech boom, optimism was high. I believed what I was told, trusting that the mutual funds I purchased would provide sufficient protection against market pain. It was only when the results didn't meet my expectations that I seriously questioned the information I had received.

Naturally, the reps rushed to tell me that I was looking at the situation incorrectly. I might have bought their slick presentations earlier, but now those presentations were belied by reality. Of course, reality is the best indicator of any strategy's success. Reality was hitting hard, and I could clearly see that the strategy I'd been pursuing wasn't working.

In good times, it's easy to be lulled into inattention. We assume that the future will be like the past. If things are good, and have been good for a while, we may conclude that they will always be good. But this can lead to complacency and a loss of focus. There's a disconnect. The problem with this approach is that when things go bad, we're unprepared, we're taken by surprise and we panic.

The only way to head off panic is to understand the risks of a course of action. When the tech bubble burst and I saw that hedging against mutual funds wasn't counteracting the losses, I realized how much of the advice I had received in my career was predicated on good times, with little understanding of the risks. That was when I understood how much more there was to learn. The fruits of this learning process are the subject of this book.

PITFALLS OF THE RETAIL INVESTMENT MODEL

As an investor, you want to trust that your financial advisor has your best interests at heart. You also want to trust that your advisor has the knowledge to serve those interests. If either of those pieces is missing, you're in trouble!

Over the years, it's become increasingly obvious to me that many advisors are constructing portfolios based on a model I call the "retail model." They're investing like individuals. And just like individuals, they're vulnerable to the emotional swings and roundabouts of the market.

Early in my career, I followed the retail model and fell into many of the traps in this book. I learned from mentors who showed me how to construct a portfolio based on the principles of that model. When I was unsure which investments to prefer, they guided me to a list of mutual funds recommended by the firm where I was working.

Naturally, I picked from the menu I was given. Naïvely, I imagined that the funds on that menu were chosen because they offered the best performance. That wasn't necessarily the case. It turned out that many of the recommended funds were the ones offering brokers the highest commission. I wasn't encouraged to ask a lot of questions, and being young and new to the business, I followed the examples set by more senior members of the practice.

I can still remember the first time my belief in the rightness of this approach was dented. A very conservative client of mine sat down with me for a meeting and began to ask pointed questions about his investments. Although this man was heavily invested in treasury bills and government bonds, he also had a portion of his portfolio in mutual funds. My firm was responsible for managing that part of his investments. At the time, the mutual funds weren't performing well.

As he began to ask me questions, I started to recognize the gaps in my knowledge. For example, he found an abbreviation in his quarterly report that read "FFO." What did FFO mean? To my chagrin, I had to admit that I didn't know. It wasn't until later that I learned it referred to funds from operations.

At the time, that conversation wasn't enough to shake my faith significantly. Nonetheless, it must have made quite an impact because I still remember it decades later. My inability to answer that client's questions or explain the performance of his investments was a clue to the limitations of the retail model.

When retail tactics yield poor results, brokers are taught to offer justifications, such as explaining that the market is volatile. In tough times, this is usually true, but it's only part of the story. Some investors—specifically institutional investors—understand how to set up their portfolios so that they limit their exposure to market volatility. We'll discuss the institutional model in the following section.

The retail investment model is centered on a buy-and-hold strategy. It's an incredibly common approach, practiced by some of the largest money managers in the world. Indeed, the two largest investment managers, in terms of amount of money managed, Barclays Global Investors and State Street Corporation, utilize this strategy.

Wikipedia defines a buy-and-hold strategy as:

> "An investment strategy where the investor buys stocks and holds them for a long time, with the goal that stocks will gradually increase in value over a long period of time. This is based on the view that in the long run, financial markets give a good rate of return, even while taking into account a degree of volatility."[1]

---

1 "Buy and Hold," Wikipedia, accessed February 17, 2020, https://en.wikipedia.org/wiki/Buy_and_hold.

Buy and hold is based on the belief that investors will never see good returns if they bail out following a decline, so the smartest approach is to hold on to their assets and wait for the market to bounce back. It's a passive strategy, not a proactive way to manage money. It's also a strategy that works for financial professionals regardless of what happens. If the investor holds on to stocks during a downturn until those stocks rebound in value, the advisor reaps an increased commission. If the investor gets antsy and sells, the advisor earns a commission on the transaction.

A corollary of this thesis is that market timing, buying when stocks are low and selling when they're high, is not a realistic goal, at least for individuals. Passive management is especially common in the equity markets where index funds track the index of a stock market, although it's becoming increasingly widespread in other financial products, such as bonds, commodities, and hedge funds. It *can* work, especially in good times, but it's a risky approach that can also yield big losses for the investor.

AN ALTERNATIVE APPROACH: THE INSTITUTIONAL MODEL

If the retail playbook is so flawed, what should investors do differently? How can you, as an investor, trust that you are getting the best possible advice? Perhaps you've consulted a broker and he's shown you a lot of flashy charts and graphs, all of which convince you that he knows exactly what he's talking about. The only problem is that you find it hard to follow his train of thought. Do you know why he's giving you the advice he's giving, or how much he'll get paid if you follow his suggestions?

The financial professionals I truly respect, some of whom you'll meet in these pages, follow a different model, known as the "institutional model." They invest like institutions, with a determination to serve something larger than the desire for immediate gratification.

As I observe the financial landscape, it seems to me that not only are most investors not getting good advice, but most don't *know* they're not getting good advice. For someone who isn't embedded in the financial world, it's hard to measure performance. What constitutes a good return and an acceptable level of risk? How would you know?

Does your advisor claim that you can beat the markets? Why would you want to do that? If you're trying to beat the markets, you'll need to have 100 percent of your money in stocks, so you'll likely be taking an unacceptable level of risk.

Besides, what's the *purpose* of beating the markets? Unless you're a thrill seeker, your authentic financial goals probably involve setting up a comfortable retirement. How much money do you need to accomplish that goal? How much risk can you comfortably absorb? These are far more important considerations than whether you can beat the market.

Ultimately, all investment is measured on portfolio performance. What's the rate of return on your investments? How well protected are you against market corrections? The bottom line is that volatility is a normal part of investing. We'd all like the market to go up every day, but we'd also like a goose that lays golden eggs. Unfortunately, the nature of markets is such that it's not going to happen.

When the markets hit a rough patch, the retail approach has little practical advice to offer. You can hold on in the hope that things will get better, or you can sell in the hope of cutting your losses. However, investing doesn't have to be that way. It's possible to acknowledge that markets are volatile *and* to invest in a way that limits your exposure to volatility.

Some brokers talk about markets as though they are cosmic forces, impenetrable to the human intellect. That's not the case. Markets are created by humans and it's possible to understand their functioning. The core message of this book is that investing is a *skill* that a good financial advisor should possess.

That doesn't mean you can make yourself invulnerable to losses. You can, however, set up your portfolio in a way that reduces risk and limits the severity of your losses in bad times, while delivering solid returns in good times.

Over the course of this book, as we unpack some of the traps that make up the retail model, we'll explore how the institutional model offers another method of constructing a portfolio.

Right now, you may be skeptical. My challenge to you at this stage is simply to keep an open mind. If you've picked up this book, I imagine it's because you'd like to invest more effectively. This may mean challenging your preconceptions and shifting your beliefs about what constitutes a good investment.

The institutional model removes a lot of the risk inherent in the retail model. It allocates assets differently, employing alternative investments, such as real estate and United States Treasury bonds. Institutional investors, such as Ray Dalio and David Swensen, consistently deliver outstanding returns, even in challenging times.

Over time, I've come to consider both Dalio and Swensen my mentors in this field. We haven't met or spoken in person, but their teachings provide an unmatched level of clarity about how investments really work. They expose many of the myths described in this book and light the way for people in my profession to follow. My hat is off to them both.

HOW I CAME TO WRITE THIS BOOK

As Winston Churchill famously said, "However beautiful the strategy, you should occasionally look at the results." I started my career accepting the retail model of investment. It was a product-focused environment, in which I learned how to deliver advice based on the needs of the market.

It was only when I confronted the poor results that my advice sometimes delivered that I began to question its fundamental premises. That led to me leaving the large brokerage firm where I worked and setting up my own practice, where I was free to put my clients' best interests first.

In the final analysis, the investment is secondary to the investor. I'm interested in knowing my clients personally, understanding what they're trying to accomplish, and meeting their financial goals. I couldn't do that within the confines of a brokerage firm, so I made the decision to become an *independent advisor*. This means I have a *fiduciary responsibility* to put my clients' interests first.

Brokers don't share this responsibility. They operate according to a *suitability responsibility*, meaning that they are free to recommend any product that suits their client's stated requirements. That's a world away from a fiduciary responsibility.

Whereas brokers are usually paid on commission, independent financial advisors operate on transparent fees, based on the quantity of assets under management. This means that brokers can be caught in a conflict of interests. If a broker is positioned to receive a 6 percent commission on a product, will he sell it to you, even if it's not in your best interests? Almost certainly. An independent financial advisor never faces this conundrum. When your assets increase in value, both you and your independent financial advisor win.

It took me years to understand the principles I espouse in this book. Following the financial collapse of 2008, I spoke with dozens of people who had been thrown into turmoil by the plunging markets. I began to wonder what I could do to help them and the thousands of others like them.

That planted the seed that eventually became this book. There's an enormous amount of bad information in the world of financial services. Worse, the average investor has no idea where to go to get good information. I've seen enough people made miserable by the vagaries of the financial markets. If this book saves even one person from staking their retirement on needlessly risky investments, it'll be worth it.

I'd like to prevent you from making the same mistakes I've made, and the same mistakes unwary investors make every day.

WHAT YOU'LL FIND IN THESE PAGES—AND WHAT YOU WON'T

If you choose to continue reading this book, you'll find a new way of looking at investing. It's a method that puts your interests first. How can you construct a portfolio that serves your real needs?

You may also find yourself questioning some orthodoxies you've previously taken for granted. The investment jungle is a dangerous place, full of pitfalls and venomous creatures. Worse, it's hard to get reliable reports on what's happening out in the wild. Financial news is very often based on fear, driving people to make hasty and unwise decisions.

For this reason, the seven chapters in this book are named after phrases you've probably heard or read. Some are partial truths. Some are distortions of the truth. None are wholly accurate. If you intend to invest pragmatically to secure your future, each one constitutes a trap that could snare you into making poor decisions. My goal is to help you steer clear of the traps.

Think of the information in these pages as a guide from someone who has spent years in the financial jungle. Someone who knows the terrain, knows where the traps are located, and who wants to see you make it through and accomplish your long-term goals.

What you won't find in this book is a get-rich-quick scheme. I can't tell you how to game the market for the purposes of making rapid gains. Indeed, I don't suggest that as a strategy. It's a surefire way to go bumbling into the nearest patch of quicksand.

Imagine that you were planning an expedition to a real jungle. You wouldn't wander in alone. You'd survey the landscape, consider your goals, and gather a team of people you trusted. That's what I suggest you do before entering the financial jungle. My aim is for this book to become your trusted companion on the journey.

Chapter One

—

TRAP ONE: HOLD ON TO THE BOAT, YOU'LL GET THROUGH THE STORM

I met Dr. Gary soon after the financial collapse of 2008. At first glance, he appeared sharply dressed and confident, the very image of a prosperous man. When I looked in his eyes, however, I saw a combination of despair and hope: despair at his recent losses and hope that I could rescue him from the situation in which he found himself.

Prior to 2008, Dr. Gary possessed approximately $1.7 million in investable assets. The markets had been on a consistent upswing and his wealth had grown in tandem with them. He felt bullish about his financial life and fully expected to see continued gains. The day I saw him, his $1.7 million was down to about $900,000. He was devastated.

Dr. Gary explained that before his investments took a nosedive, he had been on track to retire in 2009. Following the stock market crash, he had calculated that he would need to work for at least another five years to recover some of the assets he had lost. He was clearly desperate to hear me say that I could fix his problems and get him back to where he was in the space of a few months. Unfortunately, I couldn't tell him that. There was no quick fix that would restore all of his lost wealth so quickly.

Sadly, he'd dug his own financial grave. First, he was unprepared for the financial storms of 2008. His portfolio was badly rocked by those storms, just as a small rowboat would be on a tumultuous ocean, and he'd lost a significant amount of money—almost half his wealth.

Then, he compounded his mistake by selling at the bottom of the market, locking in his losses and trapping himself in a painful position. His rowboat had just about come through the storm, albeit badly damaged, but instead of setting about badly needed repairs, he sold the oars. Dr. Gary didn't know when to hold and when to sell, and as a result, he did both at the worst possible times.

A LITTLE KNOWLEDGE IS A DANGEROUS THING

"If you hold on to the boat, you'll get through the storm" is an especially insidious trap because there's some truth in it. For people who have prepared their financial craft, rough weather is no problem. Sure, it might shake them up a bit, but they won't capsize.

If Dr. Gary had set up his portfolio to reduce his risk, he could have weathered the storms of 2008 without taking serious damage. In this scenario, he likely wouldn't have become alarmed and locked in his losses by selling. He would have seen his positions gradually come back, albeit very slowly, if he'd held on to them.

What he did instead was set up a portfolio that was ideal for a rising market, but which took heavy losses when market conditions turned negative. He had a financial vessel that was ideal for sailing a calm lake on a sunny summer's day, but which was totally unsuitable for stormy weather.

As soon as the storm hit, Dr. Gary's boat was inundated, at which point he succumbed to market panic. Market panic is an emotion I've seen many times. People who are under pressure act out of a need to do something—anything!—but they don't have a clear plan. When Dr. Gary experienced market panic, he reacted by liquidating his assets.

For a professional investor working on a long timescale,

the financial crisis of 2008 was survivable. For an amateur investor such as Dr. Gary, working on the timescale of planning his own retirement, the losses he took felt calamitous.

Should you hold on to your boat when the storm hits? The answer to that question depends on the quality of your boat and the severity and duration of the storm. Dr. Gary's boat was ill-equipped to weather a storm as large as the 2008 financial crisis. When that happened, he did what any inexperienced sailor would do in terrifying circumstances: he panicked.

SHOULD YOU BUY AND HOLD?

The buy-and-hold strategy on which the idea of holding on to the boat is based relies on investors having nerves of steel when their portfolio sustains losses. This may be the case for experienced investors, but not for the average individual.

Many private investors enter into the turbulent world of the market with the expectation that their investments will steadily grow in value. They don't understand that storms and pullbacks are normal market behavior. When a storm hits, this inexperience is dangerous. You wouldn't expect an inexperienced sailor to make good decisions in gale-force winds. Inexperienced investors are no more likely to make good decisions in the teeth of a financial gale.

For this reason, I make sure that I sit my clients down at the beginning of our working relationship and discuss the inevitable storms they will encounter. When markets hit a volatile patch, I want them to be as prepared as possible. I'll help them prepare their boat and navigate through the storm, as long as they can resist the urge to sabotage the vessel.

To an extent, naiveté stems from sustained good times. When the market is good for a long time, investors forget that market corrections are natural and normal. Then, when a correction hits, those same investors panic.

In fairness, the industry does a poor job of explaining and quantifying risk. Buoyant markets provide a poor indication of risk. It's only when markets begin to perform poorly that investors truly understand how much risk they can withstand.

Advisors tend to use a 10 percent drop in value as a benchmark of what could happen in lean times. That doesn't sound like a lot and most investors are pretty comfortable with the idea that, in the worst case, their portfolio could drop 10 percent. What happens when it drops another 10 percent? And another? Those same investors suddenly find themselves, like Dr. Gary, facing huge losses, and with little idea what to do.

Should you buy and hold? The simple answer is that there's

no simple answer. If you've planned your portfolio well and you're prepared for the inevitable squalls of the market, there may be times when holding on to the boat is the smartest strategy. The major caveat here is that this doesn't apply to all portfolios, only to portfolios that are created with a clear understanding of market risk and designed to minimize exposure to negative market conditions.

If you're not prepared, you may find yourself, like Dr. Gary, clinging to the wreckage of a portfolio that seemed solidly built a few short months earlier. Should you sell? At that point, you're in a no-win situation. If you sell, you will lock in your losses. If you wait for your portfolio to recover, you may wait years.

SHORT-TERM VS. LONG-TERM VOLATILITY

Short-term fluctuations are known as headline risk. They can be triggered by comments from the chairman of the Federal Reserve Board, or even by tweets from a president. In most cases, the market bounces back quickly, sometimes as early as the following day. It's not uncommon for the Dow to fall 300 points in a day, only to rise 200 the very next day.

Larger downturns, consisting of a drop of 10 percent or more, are classified as corrections. In some years, these occur two or three times. While initially alarming, these are normal market cycles. Again, the market bounces back quickly and people forget about them.

A longer-term correction, in excess of 20 percent over a period of six to eighteen months, falls into the category of a bear market. These prolonged corrections are nerve-wracking for investors because, when they arrive, there's no end in sight. On average, bear markets come around once every five years. Smart investors construct their portfolios with bear markets in mind.

As of 2019, we've been in a bull market for more than ten years. We're significantly overdue to enter a bear market. When it happens, the correction will be more severe than most people are comfortable with. As an investor, it's important that you look ahead and build a portfolio that can withstand a bear market.

Markets change daily. Every economic year, every calendar year, is different from every previous year. Today's market is far more volatile than the market of twenty years ago. All these factors influence the way portfolios should be constructed.

Recently, the Dow dropped 800 points in a single day. I can only imagine how many investors across the country were seized by panic as they watched that day's events unfold.

What they saw was a short-term correction, causing the

value of their portfolio to plunge. Was their portfolio set up with the knowledge that these kinds of events are fairly common? Or was it set up to ride the highs of the market as long as those highs lasted? How did they respond to the loss? Did they understand that lows are inevitable and make any necessary adjustments to stay on track to meet their long-term goals? Or, did they panic and sell in the hope of minimizing their immediate losses?

Most people have strong reasons for entering the market. They want to retire in comfort thirty or forty years down the line. They want to build up a nest egg that they can leave to their children or grandchildren. Their goals are long term, but their *thinking* is short term. The important parameters of their portfolio's success are measured in years, but they try to use their monthly statements to gauge their progress.

Markets are unique in this regard. If you own a home, you don't try to assess its value every month. You're interested in the overall trajectory. What will that home be worth in two or three decades, with the mortgage paid? Very few people consider investments in the same way, even though their purpose is the same.

Storms are not a hypothetical eventuality. They *will* happen. The chances of getting through several decades of investment without seeing a major market correction are close to zero. To invest successfully, you need to determine the true goals of your portfolio. What are you investing for? How much money do you need to generate? By when? Once you know the answers to these questions, you can construct a boat that suits your objectives.

Most people, especially affluent people, take more risks than they need to. They're seduced by the prospect of high returns when they should be planning to reach their goals with minimal risk.

BUILD A BOAT THAT MEETS YOUR GOALS

Sometimes, I work with clients who are disgruntled with their returns. They tell me what they want to accomplish, and we create a portfolio that will enable them to reach those goals, with minimal risk. Then, in the middle of a bull market, they come back to me, dissatisfied that they're making 6 percent while the market's making 12 percent. I remind them of their goals and the amount of risk they told me they were willing to shoulder. Would they be happier if they were making 12 percent, only to lose half of it in the next bear market?

Investing isn't an exact science. The market is unpredictable. That very unpredictability is the reason why it's so vital to think and act strategically. I've seen retired people, living off investment returns, who find their portfolio dropping in value. That's a dangerous situation. Suddenly, they're trying to make up their losses *and* the money they're living on. They're right behind the eight ball. Worse, as retirees, they lack the income to adequately replace those funds.

The more time an investor spends in the black, the easier it is to make money, due to compounding. The money they earn becomes an asset, which they can reinvest and earn even more. The problem is that this process works in reverse. An investor who is losing money needs to return to profitability as soon as possible, to take advantage of compounding. Amazingly, few people make compounding a key part of their investment strategy.

Consider the example of two brothers, William and James. William got a jumpstart on his brother, opening his retirement account at the tender age of twenty. When he turned forty, he stopped funding the account but left it to grow tax-free at 10 percent per year.

James, meanwhile, didn't start saving until the age of forty, just as his brother was discontinuing contributions. In an attempt to offset the disadvantages of starting later, James continued paying into his account until he was sixty-five. In total, he paid into his retirement fund for twenty-five years, as opposed to William's twenty.

Both brothers invested $4,000 annually, a total of $80,000 for William and $100,000 for James. When both retired, who do you suppose had more funds available to them? That's right, the value of compounding easily outweighed the value of an extra five years of contributions.

By how much? At the age of sixty-five, William was sitting on a nest egg of $2.5 million. James had less than $400,000, an astonishing gulf of more than $2 million. Compounding is one of the most powerful investment strategies available to you. I recommend you make the most of it.

Compounding Illustrated

Year	LOW VOLATILITY		HIGH VOLATILITY	
	Growth of $100,000	Annual Return	Growth of $100,000	Annual Return
1	$110,000	10.0%	$134,000	34.0%
2	$115,500	5.0%	$121,941	−9.0%
3	$131,670	14.0%	$153,644	26.0%
4	$143,520	9.0%	$129,062	−16.0%
5	$162,178	13.0%	$169,070	31.0%
6	$165,421	2.0%	$167,380	−1.0%
7	$185,272	12.0%	$197,508	18.0%
8	$214,916	16.0%	$173,807	−12.0%
9	$227,811	6.0%	$210,306	21.0%
10	$257,426	13.0%	$227,313	8.0%
Average Return	10.0%		10.0%	
Compound Return	9.9%		8.5%	
Standard Deviation	4.5%		18.6%	

Hypothetical portfolios for illustrative purposes only.
Diversification does not assure a profit or protect against a loss.

Compounding Illustrated

Before you enter the market, it's essential that you ask yourself what you're trying to accomplish from investing. Do you want the thrill of making big returns, even if that also comes with the devastation of big losses? Or, is there a specific purpose behind your investing?

If you're looking to serve a specific purpose, be honest with yourself about what it will take to do that. Construct a portfolio—a boat—that will take you where you want to go. Don't think of the market as a magic money machine. Be realistic about the returns you can expect, even if that means adjusting your spending.

THE INSTITUTIONAL MODEL: A ROBUST BOAT

Storms are inevitable. If you build your boat carefully, however, they won't become cataclysms. The institutional model of investing, practiced by mentors of mine, such as Ray Dalio, takes a holistic view of the market. Dalio understands that markets are afflicted by stormy weather. He recognizes that a simplistic buy-and-hold strategy can't possibly prepare a portfolio for all market eventualities.

Instead, he addresses four essential elements of portfolio construction—inflation, disinflation, growth, and recession. Dalio is the founder of Bridgewater, the largest hedge fund in the world. Over many years, he has consistently delivered returns of up to 21 percent before fees. The boats he builds are so robust that he even achieved positive returns during the market collapse of 2008.

Ultimately, the idea that you should hold on to the boat and hope to come through the storm is not *completely* wrong; it's simplistic and incomplete. As I hope this chapter has shown you, there are circumstances in which it makes sense. But much depends on the quality of the boat and the severity of the storm. That's why I consider this adage a trap; it snares unwary investors into risky behavior, resulting in large losses when they find themselves attempting to withstand a major storm in a flimsy craft.

In the next chapter, we'll discuss the pitfalls of the second trap you'll encounter as you navigate the investment jungle: the belief that markets are efficient.

Chapter Two

TRAP TWO: MARKETS ARE EFFICIENT

For six years, I hosted a weekly radio show about investment and finance. One day, I received an email from a gentleman who is well-known in the technical world. We'll call him Barney.

Barney confessed that he followed my show avidly and asked for some confidential advice. He explained that he picked his stocks predominantly using technical analysis, a method he had assumed would be consistently successful.

He was surprised and concerned that his technical analysis was delivering variable results, sometimes good, sometimes poor. Barney adhered strongly to the doctrines of modern portfolio theory (MPT) and didn't understand why they weren't working as anticipated. He was convinced that markets are efficient and that they should be delivering the returns his technical analysis indicated. When he couldn't find a strong correlation between market performance and his technical analysis, he was at a loss to explain the discrepancy.

There are two basic ways to value stock: the first is *technical analysis* and the second is *fundamental analysis.*

Barney focused on the technical to the exclusion of the fundamental, using complicated analytical tools to track stock prices over time. There are several different ways to do this. One is known as a candlestick analysis. Daily stock prices are tracked on a chart that resembles a candlestick, and which many traders consider more visually appealing and easy to interpret than traditional bar charts. He used these data to track the convergence or divergence of a stock's moving average (MACD).

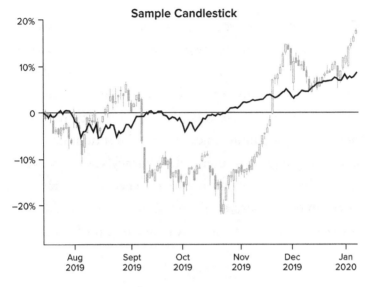

Sample Candlestick

Illustrative purposes only. Not a recommendation.

A Candlestick Chart

The MACD tracks the range in which a stock usually trades. If a stock breaks out of that range on the upside, that can indicate that it's likely to continue rising. If it drops below that range on the downside, that may mean it's liable to fall further.

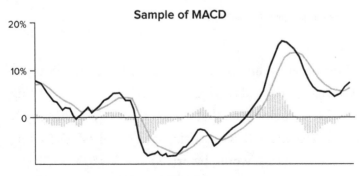

Sample of MACD

Illustrative purposes only. Not a recommendation.

A Moving Average Convergence Divergence Chart

Candlestick charts, the MACD, relative strength indicator (RSI), and other technical tools can be useful. Barney tracked a range of stocks over the course of six months in the hope of identifying those that were in line for a significant rise or fall. He was looking for stocks that were overbought and undersold, with the intention of buying and selling at the ideal moment. In Barney's mind, markets were efficient. All the information he needed was already priced into the stocks, so his technical analysis should have revealed the stocks most likely to deliver a profit or a loss.

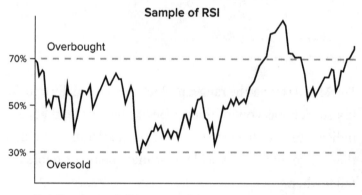

Illustrative purposes only. Not a recommendation.

A Relative Strength Indicator (RSI) Chart

Unfortunately, his strategy was flawed. If all the information Barney needed was indeed already priced into existing stocks, it would mean that markets truly were efficient. It would also mean that every single day, every stock trading on the exchange would be priced at a fair value. Clearly, this isn't the case.

When Barney reached out to me, he was losing confidence in his approach. He was so intensely focused on the technical aspects of stock analysis that he was neglecting the more fundamental aspects of stock performance. While technical analysis tracks complex patterns, fundamental analysis concentrates on the basic financial health of a company, including earnings per share, valuations, and balance sheets.

Companies that are making money are growing, those that aren't are in trouble. Technical analysis doesn't always reflect these realities, but the stock price will. Combining the two strategies generally yields better results than focusing exclusively on one.

By adding fundamental analysis to his technical expertise, Barney could have saved himself a lot of frustration and confusion. Technical analysis had become almost an article of faith to him, and he was deeply troubled when the results he saw failed to confirm its validity. Barney started with a theory and became perturbed when reality didn't fit his theory. A much smarter approach would have been to start with reality and ask himself how to explain what he saw.

WHAT IS MODERN PORTFOLIO THEORY?

Throughout this book, we'll contrast modern portfolio theory with the institutional model of investing. Therefore, it's important to dive into an explanation of what MPT is, where it came from, and how it is believed to work. Although MPT is almost ubiquitous in investing circles, it's actually quite a limited model.

MPT is a mathematical approach to understanding markets. Clearly, markets change over time. MPT examines those changes in terms of returns, profit and loss, and risk. In its more complex incarnations, MPT also presents measures of portfolio performance that combine risk and return.

The primary objective of MPT is to determine approaches to investing that will maximize returns and minimize risk. Return, for example, is measured as a percentage of change. Did the investment go up or down, and by what percentage did it change? Risk is measured by comparing the distribution of returns with the average performance of the market. The idea is that a savvy investor utilizing MPT should be able to predict results and make good investments, resulting in a growing portfolio and solid returns.

MPT originated in the classroom of Harry Markowitz, who is widely recognized as the father of MPT. In 1952, Markowitz asked his students whether it was possible to predict the movements of the market and set up a better portfolio based on those predictions. Their work became MPT, which was later refined by William Sharpe in 1964.

Nowadays, MPT is so well-established that it has been woven into investing orthodoxy and it's sometimes assumed to be universally true. That's absolutely not the case. MPT is a theory about how the market works. If it were scientific fact, experiments would demonstrate its accuracy time and time again. That's not at all the case.

MPT rests on four basic assumptions. The first, which we're discussing in this chapter, is that **markets are efficient.** The second, which will be the subject of the next chapter, is that **risk and volatility are the same.** The third assumption of MPT, which we'll cover in chapter 4, is that **correlations are static.**

The fourth and final assumption is that **people act rationally** in the world of investing. That assumption is so obviously off the mark that I don't think it needs a chapter to itself. If you've ever seen how people behave during a market panic, you'll know that whatever is driving their behavior, it is certainly not rationality!

WHY MARKETS AREN'T EFFICIENT

The idea that markets are efficient is a trap that snares many unwary investors. In academic circles, there's a roughly even split between those who support MPT and those who question it. In case you want to dive into the academic side of the argument, I recommend *The New Finance: The*

Case Against Efficient Markets, by Robert Haugen. For our purposes, let's explore the three versions of the efficient markets hypothesis (EMH): the strong, the semi-strong, and the weak.

THE STRONG VERSION

The strong version of EMH asserts that MPT is highly accurate and that all information including insider information is already priced into the stock. Therefore, the price of a stock reflects its real value and the most effective strategy is to choose a stock that's liable to rise, buy it, and hold onto it. The implication is that there's no way to make a profit on a stock over and above a gradual rise in value that will be reflected by the market.

Anyone who has studied the workings of the stock market knows this isn't the case. Some stocks are overpriced while others are underpriced. Some rise based on nothing more concrete than enthusiasm and confidence—the dot-com boom was a perfect example of this—while others fall due to speculation or alarm.

The strongest version of EMH rejects the idea that insiders are privy to information that's denied to the average investor, a claim that's patently untrue. Insider trading is a reality of the market—people are constantly looking for tips about which stocks will rise and which will fall. Indeed,

Martha Stewart famously went to jail for her participation in insider trading.

THE SEMI-STRONG VERSION

The semi-strong version of EMH acknowledges that it would theoretically be possible for insiders to gain an advantage through nonpublic information but denies that this is a concern. Insider trading is illegal. When a firm undergoes an initial public offering (IPO), there are procedures in place to prevent information leaking from one part of a brokerage firm to another.

The point is that insider information *does* exist, and it *could* be used to gain additional profits, but there are rules and regulations to prevent insider information being leaked. In practice, insiders can't gain an advantage from information denied to outside investors. For advocates of the semi-strong EMH position, once again the smartest investment strategy is to buy and hold.

THE WEAK VERSION

The third and weakest version of EMH claims that analyzing stocks based on historical performance, or using technical or fundamental analysis, will not yield additional profits. According to those who believe in this hypothesis, both technical analysis and fundamental analysis are redundant because they provide the analyst with no advantages that couldn't be gained from looking at the stock price. Past performance is not a guide to future performance.

The problem with all three of these versions is that they don't account for anomalies. Anything that falls outside the purview of MPT is explained away or ignored. Those who believe in MPT would rather discard information that doesn't fit their theory than adapt their theory to fit the information.

It would be wonderful to believe that the market is transparent and that any amateur investor can interpret publicly available information to understand the true state of the market. Unfortunately, that's not the case. Even many professionals, who adhere to MPT, were at a loss to explain the financial collapse of 2008. The portfolios they set up in accordance with MPT tumbled by as much as 40 to 70 percent, and their clients suffered badly.

Fortunately, there is an alternative to MPT. The institutional model, which we've touched on in both the introduction and chapter 1, doesn't rely on the belief that markets are efficient. Instead, it assumes that markets are unpredictable and risky. Institutional investors construct portfolios based on this understanding, with the intention of maximizing gains while minimizing risk.

HOW DOES THE INSTITUTIONAL MODEL WORK?

The majority of retail investors pour money into the stock market, reasoning that this is the best opportunity for them to make big, quick returns. The problem with this approach is that the stock market is one of the riskiest investment arenas. Sure, some stocks appreciate rapidly, but many others drop just as fast. There are few safeguards, so there's almost no limit to how much the unwary investor can lose.

In an effort to hedge against risk, many retail investors, whether they're working with advisors or going it alone, follow advice they've heard or read about asset allocation. For example, they invest 60 percent of their funds in the stock market and 40 percent in lower-risk, lower-return investments, such as bonds.

The idea of spreading risk through different asset classes is a good one, but the execution is poor. With 60 percent of investable assets in stocks, the potential for volatility is huge. This can lead to big wins. It can also lead to crushing defeats. In future chapters, we'll examine the dynamics of this approach in more detail, explaining why it's a poor strategy for anyone planning for the long term.

Institutional investors significantly reduce the percentage of assets invested in stocks. For example, an institutional investor might put 20 to 30 percent of the assets under their management into stocks, with 40 percent in bonds, and the remaining 30 to 40 percent in commodities, real estate, gold, and other alternative investments.

Remember, the institutional model is based on investing like an institution. The purpose is to build a significant endowment over decades, even centuries. What good does it do for an institution to win big on the stock market, knowing that bull and bear markets always balance out eventually? If not this year, those gains will be wiped out next year, or ten years hence. That's the way it goes in a volatile environment.

Once again, the key question is: what do you want to achieve? Do you want to take a punt on beating the markets? You can do that, and you may succeed, at least for a time. Like casinos, however, the house always wins in the end. Beating the market *consistently* over decades is extremely difficult, and it's not a stable strategy to rely on when planning your retirement.

Ray Dalio, who we discussed in the previous chapter, employs the institutional model. David Swensen, who manages funds for Yale, also invests this way. Their job is to deliver consistent low-risk returns for high-net-worth individuals and institutions, year after year after year. Dalio and Swensen don't need to beat the market. They need to protect and grow the investments of the people and organizations that trust them with their money.

Retail investors often rely on hope. They hope that if they put their money in the right place, they can grow it quickly. Institutional investors understand that when managing substantial assets, hope isn't a good strategy. They need to be constantly aware of the risks of a substantial loss.

Although the possibility of a big win is seductive, I don't believe most people are truly looking to beat the market. They just want to invest their money and see it grow at a fair rate. Financial advertisers claim that investing is simple. In reality, that's not the case.

DALBAR is an independent organization that studies investor behavior. Every year, it brings out a report. According to the 2018 DALBAR study, the average investor garners annual returns of 2.52 percent, while those who work with a skilled professional can expect to roughly double that return, bringing in returns of approximately 4.8 percent.

Dalbar Study

	20 Year	10 Year	5 Year	3 Year	12 Month
Average Equity Fund Investor (%)	5.29	4.88	10.93	8.12	20.64
Average Fixed Income Fund Investor (%)	0.44	0.48	−0.40	−0.05	1.52
Average Asset Allocation Fund Investor (%)	2.58	2.52	5.41	3.85	10.08
Inflation (%)	2.15	1.64	1.48	1.71	2.11
S&P 500 (%)	7.20	8.50	15.79	11.41	21.83
Bloomberg-Barclays Aggregate Treasury Index (%)	4.60	3.31	1.27	1.40	2.31

Comparing Investments (Credit: DALBAR QAIB Report 2018)

As the title of this book suggests, diving into financial markets is similar to planning an expedition to the jungle. Both are unfamiliar terrain, riddled with dangers for the unwary. Anyone who enters a jungle without a trained guide is asking for trouble. The same is true of anyone who wanders into the financial jungle unprepared.

Yet most people spend more time planning their upcoming vacation than planning their retirement. They believe the messages they see and hear in the media, invest their money without oversight, and fall into one of the traps detailed in this book.

THE ANTIDOTE TO TECHNICAL ANALYSIS

Remember Barney from the beginning of this chapter? Barney was convinced that with enough analysis, he could predict the movements of the market. He made one of the classic mistakes of the retail investor by believing that markets are efficient, and behaving as though this were true. When he contacted me, he was confused and alarmed by his lackluster results.

Here's an example of how unpredictable the markets can be. During the 2008 financial collapse, General Motors took a $12 billion loan from American taxpayers. Stockholders in the company, who would otherwise have suffered catastrophic losses, were reimbursed. Bondholders, on the other hand, lost their money.

This is a reversal of the usual hierarchy. In most scenarios, bondholders take precedence over stockholders. Not even an experienced investor could have predicted that GM would bail out stockholders while abandoning bondholders. Certainly, no technical analysis could have foreseen that outcome.

David Swensen operates at the opposite end of the scale. He knows that markets aren't efficient, and his investment strategy reflects this fact. Over many years, he has consistently delivered strong returns, averaging 14 percent over several decades. The Yale endowment fund under his management has grown from $3 billion to $30 billion.

David Swensen's book, *Unconventional Success*, outlines the issues most retail investors face and explains how the institutional position resolves these issues. He speaks from experience, with authority, about the potential and pitfalls of investing, and the keys to doing so successfully.

In the next chapter, we'll tackle another pervasive trap you're sure to encounter as you traverse the financial jungle: the belief that risk and volatility are the same.

Chapter Three

TRAP THREE: RISK AND VOLATILITY ARE THE SAME

Back in 2009, in the aftermath of the financial collapse, I met with a couple who had taken a radical approach to investing, one which they thought allowed them to circumnavigate the most common problems faced by investors. We'll call them Gavin and Barbara.

When they entered my office, I began to ask them questions, so I could understand the reasons why they wanted to meet me. I inquired as to why they had come, their investment history, and how familiar they were with investing. Instead of explaining their problems and requesting my advice, Gavin started telling me, with an air of self-satisfaction, that he had got out of the market completely, just before it had begun to turn downward. It seemed that he wanted to convey how smart he was.

When I pressed him for more details, he grinned and told me that he had sold all of his stocks and mutual funds, taken around $250,000 from an IRA, and invested in gold. At the time, gold was selling for about $2,500 an ounce and Gavin believed firmly in the advice of experts and pundits who were saying it would rise to $5,000, doubling his money.

As I listened, he explained his theory that the dollar would soon collapse, destroying the preeminent position of the United States and crashing our stock markets. In his view, gold was his insurance policy.

Gavin was in his midfifties and I asked him about his retirement plan. He had another ten years in the workplace before he was ready to retire, and I wanted to know how he saw that scenario panning out. He looked at me as though I was crazy and said, "I'll sell some of my gold to fund my retirement, of course."

In his mind, that was a sound plan. Unfortunately, he was betting heavily on some highly questionable assumptions. First, that the price of gold would continue to rise to the point where his returns would be significantly better than if he'd stayed in the stock market. Second, that if the dollar collapsed, gold would be the preferred currency going forward. I decided to challenge him on those assumptions.

"Okay," I said, "let's play devil's advocate. Let's imagine that the dollar collapses, the stock market crashes, and you have a pile of gold. Let's also imagine that I have a 500-gallon storage tank of gasoline, and in a world of increasing scarcity, you want to buy twenty gallons of gasoline so you can run your car."

He nodded at me, engaging with the scenario I was sharing.

"You come to me wanting twenty gallons of gas," I continued. "What will you give me in exchange for that gas?" When he said that he would offer gold, I responded, "I don't care. What good will gold do me?"

"What do you mean you don't care?" he asked.

I explained that in a world with no stock market and a worthless dollar, I'd rather have gasoline than gold. At this point, Barbara looked at me, then back at him. Clearly, she was weighing up whether he was smart or crazy.

Since 2009, gold prices dropped to around $1,200 an ounce, although they recently rebounded slightly to close to $1,500. If he's still holding onto gold that he bought at $2,500 an ounce, he's lost a lot of money.

I see a lot of people who pursue strategies without fully understanding the assumptions—and therefore the risks—underlying those strategies. Our friend wanted to escape the volatility of the stock market and, in doing so, confused volatility with risk. He thought that by shifting his investment into a less volatile commodity, he was reducing his risk. Instead, he placed himself in a losing position.

THE DIFFERENCE BETWEEN RISK AND VOLATILITY

There are many kinds of risks in investing. There's interest rate risk, default risk, and market risk, for example, all of which have unique characteristics. To accurately assess the potential downside of an investment, it's important to understand the worst-case scenario. That means defining the risk. Not all risk is created equal.

Every investment comes with risk, and it's important that investors understand the risk they're taking on prior to entering into an agreement. In previous chapters, we've discussed the fact that some brokers ask clients how comfortable they feel losing 10 percent of their capital. To many people 10 percent seems like a reasonable percentage. They feel that they could handle that level of loss.

Now, what happens when we put numbers to that 10 percent? Let's say that a client has $300,000 to invest. If they lose 10 percent of that money, they'll be down $30,000. Does that seem palatable? Probably not.

To understand the risk inherent in a particular type of investment, we need to assess the amount of money an investor could lose and the *probability* of that loss. If the amount of money at stake is high, investors will usually only tolerate a very small probability of loss, whereas if the amount of money at stake is relatively low, investors may tolerate a higher probability of loss. Each type of security comes with its own type of systemic risk. The smart investor will understand those risks.

Risk, however, is not the same as volatility. As James Mai eloquently says, "One of the great misconceptions of the investing public is equating risk with volatility."[2] It's easy to assume that the most volatile investments are the riskiest. This may sometimes be the case, but not always. Conflating the two is dangerous.

If risk and volatility aren't the same, then what is volatility? In simple terms, it's the degree to which an investment fluctuates in value. Usually, this is calculated with reference to standard deviation, meaning how much a given investment departs from the average.[3]

---

2   Quoted in Schwager, Jack D., *Hedge Fund Market Wizards: How Winning Traders Win* (New York: John Wiley & Sons, 2012), 259.

3   The formula for calculating geometric return is $(1+R1)(1+R2)(1+R3)(\text{etc.}) \, 1/2n - 1$.

To cement the point, let's look at an example. Stock in Company A rises 15 percent in April, another 5 percent in May, and a further 10 percent in June. In total, the stock has risen by 32.8 percent across the three months. Great, right? It's also risen at wildly differing rates across those three months, from 5 percent to 15 percent. The stock is highly volatile but has delivered excellent returns.

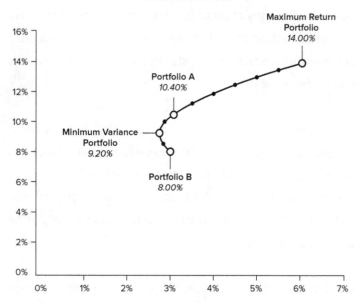

Efficient Frontier

Optimal Risk-Adjusted Returns (Credit: www.thismatters.com)

Let's look at what could happen if the stock began to decline. Imagine that Company A hits a speed bump in July. In August, the stock declines by 15 percent. The same happens in September, and again in October. By the beginning of November, the stock has declined by 38.6 percent from its June high. That's a serious loss.

Across the three months of August to October, however, the stock has exhibited low volatility. It has declined by a steady 15 percent, not deviating at all from the mean, although it's unlikely that this lack of volatility will be much consolation to anyone invested in the stock!

Volatility *can* be correlated with risk, but not necessarily. Do investors really care about volatility? Not much, compared with how much they care about their returns or losses. When people confuse volatility and risk, they may make unwise investments and suffer painful consequences.

HOW TO CONTROL YOUR RISK

If selecting low volatility stocks doesn't guarantee low risk, then what does? The key is calculating risk and selecting a range of investments that spread and minimize risk.

A standard portfolio based on MPT consists of roughly 50 percent stocks and 50 percent bonds. At first glance, this may look like a good ratio of potential risk to potential reward. What this simple division of investment fails to reveal, however, is that stocks are almost five times riskier than bonds. With 50 percent of a portfolio in stocks and 50 percent in bonds, 95 percent of total risk is concentrated in the stocks. In terms of *dollar allocation*, the portfolio looks balanced. In terms of risk, it certainly isn't.

Fine Tuning Table - S&P 500 Equity Portfolio

No Mgmt Fee. Fund expense ratios subtracted from all portfolios except S&P 500 Index.

Year	100% Bonds	10/90	20/80	30/70	40/60	50/50	60/40
1970	14.8%	13.8%	12.8%	11.8%	10.7%	9.6%	8.5%
1971	7.7%	8.4%	9.1%	9.8%	10.5%	11.2%	11.8%
1972	4.8%	6.1%	7.5%	8.9%	10.3%	11.7%	13.1%
1973	4.5%	2.5%	0.5%	-1.5%	-3.4%	-5.3%	-7.3%
1974	7.5%	3.8%	0.2%	-3.4%	-6.9%	-10.4%	-13.8%
1975	7.7%	10.5%	13.3%	16.2%	19.1%	22.0%	25.0%
1976	9.7%	11.1%	12.6%	14.0%	15.4%	16.8%	18.2%
1977	3.1%	2.1%	1.0%	0.0%	-1.1%	-2.1%	-3.2%
1978	2.6%	3.1%	3.6%	4.0%	4.4%	4.8%	5.2%
1979	7.1%	8.2%	9.3%	10.5%	11.6%	12.7%	13.8%
1980	7.5%	9.9%	12.4%	14.9%	17.4%	19.9%	22.4%
1981	10.8%	9.1%	7.5%	5.9%	4.3%	2.7%	1.1%
1982	23.7%	23.6%	23.5%	23.3%	23.1%	22.9%	22.6%
1983	8.2%	9.6%	10.9%	12.3%	13.8%	15.2%	16.6%
1984	14.0%	13.3%	12.5%	11.8%	11.0%	10.2%	9.4%
1985	16.5%	18.0%	19.6%	12.1%	22.7%	24.2%	25.8%
1986	12.1%	12.8%	13.5%	14.2%	14.9%	15.5%	16.2%
1987	4.1%	4.7%	5.2%	5.5%	5.8%	6.0%	6.1%
1988	6.1%	7.2%	8.2%	9.3%	10.3%	11.4%	12.4%
1989	12.0%	13.9%	15.8%	17.7%	19.6%	21.5%	23.5%
1990	10.6%	9.3%	7.9%	6.6%	5.2%	3.8%	2.4%
1991	15.3%	16.8%	18.3%	19.9%	21.4%	22.9%	24.4%
1992	7.2%	7.3%	7.3%	7.4%	7.4%	7.4%	7.5%
1993	9.7%	9.8%	9.8%	9.8%	9.9%	9.9%	9.9%
1994	-3.2%	-2.7%	-2.3%	-1.8%	-1.4%	-0.9%	-0.5%
1995	16.6%	18.5%	20.5%	22.5%	24.6%	26.7%	28.8%
1996	3.1%	5.0%	6.9%	8.8%	10.7%	12.7%	14.7%
1997	7.0%	9.5%	12.0%	14.5%	17.1%	19.7%	22.4%
1998	8.1%	10.2%	12.3%	14.5%	16.5%	18.6%	20.7%
1999	-0.5%	1.6%	3.6%	5.7%	7.8%	9.9%	12.1%
2000	11.7%	9.6%	7.4%	5.3%	3.2%	1.1%	-1.0%
2001	8.1%	6.2%	4.2%	2.2%	0.2%	-1.8%	-3.8%
2002	12.4%	8.7%	5.0%	1.4%	-2.1%	-5.6%	-9.1%
2003	3.5%	5.8%	8.2%	10.7%	13.1%	15.6%	18.1%
2004	4.0%	4.7%	5.4%	6.1%	6.8%	7.4%	8.1%
2005	1.8%	2.2%	2.5%	28%	3.1%	3.4%	3.7%
2006	3.0%	4.2%	5.5%	6.7%	8.0%	9.2%	10.5%
2007	9.3%	9.0%	8.6%	8.3%	7.9%	7.5%	7.1%
2008	8.1%	2.7%	-2.4%	-7.4%	-12.2%	-16.8%	-21.2%
2009	2.0%	4.4%	6.8%	9.3%	11.7%	14.1%	16.6%
2010	5.5%	6.6%	7.7%	8.7%	9.7%	10.7%	11.6%
2011	8.0%	7.5%	7.0%	6.4%	5.9%	5.3%	4.7%
2012	3.4%	4.7%	5.9%	7.3%	8.4%	9.7%	10.9%
2013	-3.6%	-0.4%	2.8%	6.2%	9.6%	13.1%	16.7%
2014	3.4%	4.4%	5.4%	6.4%	7.5%	8.5%	9.5%
2015	0.8%	0.9%	1.0%	1.1%	1.2%	1.3%	1.3%
2016	1.8%	2.8%	3.8%	4.8%	5.9%	6.9%	7.9%
2017	1.9%	3.7%	5.6%	7.5%	9.4%	11.4%	13.4%
2018	0.6%	0.2%	-0.2%	-0.6%	-1.1%	-1.6%	-2.2%
Annualized Return	7.0%	7.5%	7.9%	8.3%	8.7%	9.0%	9.4%
Standard Deviation	4.1%	4.1%	4.7%	5.6%	6.7%	8.0%	9.3%
Worst 3 Months	-4.6%	-4.7%	-6.3%	-9.2%	-12.4%	-15.4%	-18.4%
Worst 6 Months	-4.1%	-4.7%	-8.1%	-13.1%	-17.8%	-22.2%	-26.5%
Worst 12 Months	-3.6%	-3.3%	-8.6%	-13.7%	-18.5%	-23.2%	-27.6%
Worst 36 Months Annualized	0.2%	1.6%	1.7%	-0.4%	-2.6%	-4.7%	6.8%
Worst 60 Months Annualized	0.7%	2.2%	2.3%	1.2%	0.1%	-1.0%	2.1%
Worst Draw Down	-4.7%	-5.5%	-8.9%	-14.2%	-19.8%	-25.9%	-31.7%

Fine Tuning Table - S&P 500 Equity Portfolio (Continued)

No Mgmt Fee. Fund expense ratios subtracted from all portfolios except S&P 500 Index.

Year	70/30	80/20	90/10	100% S&P 500	S&P 500 Index
1970	7.4%	6.3%	5.1%	3.9%	4.0%
1971	12.4%	13.0%	13.6%	14.2%	14.3%
1972	14.5%	15.9%	17.4%	18.9%	19.0%
1973	-9.2%	-11.0%	-12.9%	-14.8%	-14.7%
1974	-17.1%	-20.3%	-23.5%	-26.5%	-26.5%
1975	27.9%	31.0%	34.0%	37.1%	37.2%
1976	19.6%	21.0%	22.3%	23.7%	23.8%
1977	-4.2%	-5.2%	-6.3%	-7.3%	7.2%
1978	5.5%	5.9%	6.2%	6.5%	6.6%
1979	15.0%	16.1%	17.2%	18.3%	18.4%
1980	24.9%	27.4%	29.8%	32.3%	32.4%
1981	-0.4%	-2.0%	-3.5%	-5.0%	-4.9%
1982	22.3%	22.0%	21.7%	21.3%	21.4%
1983	18.0%	19.5%	20.9%	22.4%	22.5%
1984	8.6%	7.8%	7.0%	6.2%	6.3%
1985	27.3%	28.9%	30.5%	32.0%	32.2%
1986	16.7%	17.3%	17.8%	18.4%	18.5%
1987	6.0%	5.8%	5.5%	5.1%	5.2%
1988	13.5%	14.6%	15.6%	16.7%	16.8%
1989	25.4%	27.4%	29.4%	31.4%	31.5%
1990	1.0%	-0.4%	-1.8%	-3.2%	-3.1%
1991	25.9%	27.4%	28.9%	30.3%	30.5%
1992	7.5%	7.5%	7.5%	7.5%	7.6%
1993	9.9%	9.9%	10.0%	10.0%	10.1%
1994	0.1%	0.4%	0.8%	1.2%	1.3%
1995	30.9%	33.0%	35.2%	37.4%	37.6%
1996	16.7%	18.7%	20.8%	22.8%	23.0%
1997	25.0%	27.7%	30.5%	33.2%	33.4%
1998	22.7%	24.6%	26.6%	28.5%	28.6%
1999	14.3%	16.5%	18.7%	20.9%	21.0%
2000	-3.1%	-5.1%	-7.2%	-9.2%	-9.1%
2001	-5.9%	-7.9%	-9.9%	-12.0%	-11.9%
2002	-12.5%	-15.8%	-19.0%	-22.2%	-22.1%
2003	20.7%	23.3%	25.9%	28.6%	28.7%
2004	8.8%	9.4%	10.1%	10.8%	10.9%
2005	4.0%	4.3%	4.5%	4.8%	4.9%
2006	11.8%	13.1%	14.4%	15.7%	15.8%
2007	6.7%	6.3%	5.8%	5.4%	5.5%
2008	-25.4%	-28.5%	-33.3%	-37.1%	-37.0%
2009	19.0%	21.5%	23.9%	26.3%	26.5%
2010	12.5%	13.4%	14.2%	14.9%	15.1%
2011	4.0%	3.4%	2.7%	2.0%	2.1%
2012	12.2%	13.4%	14.6%	15.9%	16.0%
2013	20.5%	24.3%	28.2%	32.3%	32.4%
2014	10.5%	11.5%	12.6%	13.6%	13.7%
2015	1.3%	1.3%	1.3%	1.3%	1.4%
2016	8.9%	9.9%	10.9%	11.8%	12.0%
2017	15.4%	17.5%	19.6%	21.7%	21.8%
2018	-2.7%	-3.3%	-3.9%	-4.5%	-4.4%
Annualized Return	9.7%	9.9%	10.2%	10.4%	10.5%
Standard Deviation	10.7%	12.2%	13.6%	15.1%	15.1%
Worst 3 Months	-21.3%	-24.2%	-27.0%	-29.7%	-29.6%
Worst 6 Months	-30.6%	-34.6%	-38.3%	-41.9%	-41.8%
Worst 12 Months	-30.8%	-35.9%	-39.7%	-43.4%	-43.3%
Worst 36 Months Annualized	-9.0%	-11.1%	-13.6	-16.2%	-16.1%
Worst 60 Months Annualized	-3.3%	-4.4%	-5.6	-6.7%	-6.6%
Worst Draw Down	-37.0%	-42.0%	-46.7	-51.0%	50.9%

Fine Tuning Table (Used by permission of the Merriman Foundation)

There's a reason why this type of allocation is so popular. It's supported by MPT, which advocates dividing assets up and allocating a percentage to different asset classes. But it fails to take into account the different levels of risk associated with different types of investment.

At times, MPT appears to have the answers. There have been long periods where assigning 50 percent of a portfolio to stocks and 50 percent to bonds would have delivered solid returns. Unfortunately, risks alter constantly. A relatively safe portfolio can quickly become a risky one. The unwary investor, or one who takes their eye off the ball, can quickly find themselves playing a losing game.

The institutional model takes into account both risk and volatility, assigning assets accordingly. Generally speaking, this means limiting exposure to the United States stock market to no more than 30 percent of a portfolio. Managed skillfully, this strategy can deliver good returns with relatively low risk.

Over the course of four decades, it's possible to see where risk and volatility meet, and where they diverge. Bonds are significantly less volatile than stocks, fluctuating approximately 4 percent above or below their mean. In the same timeframe, overall stock volatility is 15.1 percent, meaning stocks fluctuated on average 15.1 percent above or below their mean.

Going all the way back to 1970, the worst three months in history across the S&P 500 is a decline of 29.6 percent. Over six months, the worst decline is 41.8 percent. The worst twelve-month performance is a decline of 43.4 percent. Clearly, the stock market is a volatile place. If risk and volatility were the same, we'd expect that volatility to be correlated with high returns. Is it? Not necessarily.

Between 1970 and 2017, an average portfolio made up of 70 percent stocks and 30 percent bonds delivers a return of 9.7 percent, at a standard deviation of 10.7. The degree of fluctuation, and therefore the chance that the portfolio will under deliver, is relatively high.

Contrast that with a portfolio made up of 30 percent stocks and 70 percent bonds across the same time period. This delivers an average return of 8.3 percent with a standard deviation of a mere 5.6 percent. The return drops by 1.4 percentage points, while the volatility drops 5.1 percentage points. The second portfolio delivers returns that are almost as strong as the first, with a much lower chance that it will suddenly drop or fluctuate dramatically in value. It is much less risky than the first.

Some people argue that dancing with volatility is a risk worth taking. Why? Because, they say, investors are rewarded for investing in more volatile commodities. As the above calculation demonstrates, however, it's possible to reduce volatility considerably without significantly affecting returns.

TAKING THE LONGER VIEW

As we've seen, Gavin invested in gold thinking that it was less volatile than the stock market, and even the dollar itself.

He was so scared of a stock market catastrophe that he embedded himself in a whole different category of risk. The risk that there would *not* be a catastrophe, and his gold would remain at about the same level or decrease in price, and the corresponding risk that in a post-crash version of the United States, he would be stuck with a lot of gold that was no use to him and not valuable to anyone else.

The whole goal of major media outlets is to promote an emotion, usually fear. Fear drives people to make poorly considered decisions in an effort to assuage risk and volatility. Volatility is one form of risk, but it's not the only form. Assuming that they are the same leads to some questionable investing decisions. The most likely is that you will invest too heavily in stocks, thinking that you will be rewarded for taking on volatility.

As a long-term investor, you can minimize your market risk by taking a longer view and calculating the probable value of your investments in ten, twenty, or thirty years. Every single day, the markets go up, often by as much as three hundred points, and occasionally by even more. If you try to calculate your risks based on the daily movement of stocks, you will soon be stressed and exhausted.

When I'm constructing a portfolio for a client, I'm interested in how their investments will look when they retire, not how excited they'll be when they open next month's statement. Will a company be more viable in five years than it is today? If so, it doesn't much matter what happens in two months, six months, or even a year. If the company's stock goes through a volatile period that doesn't impact the overall financials, the total investment may continue to be quite safe.

Imagine that you were setting off on a long-term expedition to the jungle. Would you take two months' worth of fresh fruit, vegetables, and meat? Of course not. You'd invest in three years' worth of tinned food—and several spare tin openers. It's no good to you to feast for a couple of months, then starve. You want to come out of the jungle in good shape. Yet, too many people take a short-term view when planning their investments, even when their overall goal is to build a nest egg for their retirement. They behave like there's no tomorrow, chasing instant gratification and panicking when the markets hit a blip.

The wise course of action is to choose investments that

offer solid returns, not to chase high returns at potentially excessive cost. Gavin and Barbara tried to beat volatility by pouring their money into gold. But there is a way to limit the impact of volatility by planning a portfolio that will ride the fluctuations in the market.

In the next chapter, we'll investigate the phenomena of correlations—how closely particular investments track the markets. As you'll recall, MPT claims that correlations are static. In fact, they change all the time.

Chapter Four

TRAP FOUR: CORRELATIONS ARE STATIC

In the mid-nineties, a gentleman named Jacob came into my office. Jacob was in his seventies, with a good-sized portfolio of stocks. In total, his assets were worth well over $2 million.

Jacob explained that he had worked most of his life in the same field, and anytime he received a raise or a bonus, he used the additional money to purchase stocks. His investments followed a pattern. He liked utility stocks because he believed that they were a safe investment, and also because they paid out dividends. Jacob took a conservative approach to investment, reaping large returns that he used to supplement his retirement.

At the time I met him, however, Jacob was concerned at the stagnation of his portfolio. The market had shifted against utility stocks, and the positions that had traditionally served him well were no longer as reliable as they used to be. His stocks were dropping in value and he was unsure what to do about it.

The bigger problem was that Jacob had become emotionally attached to his portfolio. He was unwilling to change his strategy, leaving him trapped by his own portfolio. Instead of his money working for him, it was working against him.

This is fairly common in the supposedly rational world of finance, especially among people who have received an inheritance from their parents. The positions they have inherited represent an emotional connection, and they become unwilling to sell any of those positions. As a result, they become a prisoner of their investments.

Jacob and I talked at length about potential strategies. With utilities fading, I advised him to liquidate some of his positions. He resisted, both due to his emotional attachment and because he didn't want to pay the capital gains tax he would incur through selling.

I explained that with the growth and dividends he had seen over the years, the capital gains were a minor concern. At the time, technology stocks were coming to the fore. Had he taken the plunge and moved some of his money from utilities to technology, he would likely have seen significant growth.

Jacob was unwilling to credit this idea. In his mind, utilities had always performed well for him and would continue to do so. He was alarmed by the declines, but he wasn't willing to concede that he needed a different strategy. He believed that the stocks would surely bounce back.

Without stating it explicitly, Jacob took the position that correlations were static. If utility stocks were once a good investment, they would *always* be a good investment. He couldn't see the rise of technology stocks as anything more than a small, incidental movement.

Jacob wasn't in a terrible position. He still received dividends and his overall portfolio was substantial. His mindset, however, was flawed. The only constant in markets is change. By failing to recognize this, Jacob fell victim to the fourth of our seven traps.

HOW CORRELATIONS WORK

As a general rule, investments either move in line with the market or in the opposite direction. When the market goes up, some stocks go up, while others go down. Other investments, such as real estate, may be positively correlated with the market—meaning that they rise in value when the market goes up—or negatively correlated, meaning that they increase in value when the market goes down.

More confusingly, correlations change all the time. According to MPT, this shouldn't be the case. Correlations should be static. They should always stay the same. That sounds great in theory, but it isn't borne out by the markets. What will you believe? A convincing theory, or reality? Making investing decisions in the belief that correlations are static gets investors into a lot of trouble.

Let's break down exactly what correlation means. For this discussion, we'll use the Pearson model, the most commonly used in financial circles.

Correlation is the strength of a relationship based on two variables. When x happens, how likely is it that y will happen? That variable is the correlation coefficient. In simple terms, the Pearson model measures both the **strength** and the **direction** of a linear relationship between two variables. For example, how closely is a particular stock's value tied to the overall direction of the market, and in what direction? Does it go down when the market goes down? By the same amount?

We calculate this correlation coefficient by taking the standard deviation and dividing it by the difference. In most cases, the number is somewhere between negative one—indicating an inverse correlation—and positive one.

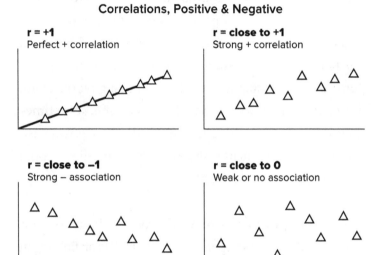

Correlations, Positive & Negative

r = +1
Perfect + correlation

r = close to +1
Strong + correlation

r = close to –1
Strong – association

r = close to 0
Weak or no association

How Correlations Are Calculated (Credit: Boston University Public Health)

The problem comes when every stock in a portfolio is positively correlated or negatively correlated with the market. Imagine someone who has forty stocks, all of which tend to move in the same direction as the market. In some cases, the correlation may be strong—let's say .8. In others, it may be weak—perhaps .2. In every case, however, the relationship between the stock and the market is a positive one. What happens when the market undergoes a sudden correction? All those positively correlated stocks drop with it.

THE DIFFERENCE BETWEEN CORRELATION AND CAUSATION

When people become confused about correlation, they often extend that confusion into the belief that correlation and causation are the same phenomena. This belief has been a flaw in human thinking since the first tribes performed rain dances in the hope of being blessed with life-giving water. Sometimes the rains came, sometimes they didn't. Did people conclude that the dances were useless? Or did they conclude that when the rains didn't come, their execution was at fault?

You may think that we've moved beyond such superstition. If so, consider the star right fielder who insists on fielding in his lucky glove, all because he once took an amazing catch while wearing it. The lucky glove didn't *cause* him to take the brilliant catch, but now he's emotionally invested in the correlation. What happens if he loses his lucky glove? He's convinced that he will perform poorly. That belief may be so powerful that it becomes self-fulfilling, and the fielder *actually does perform poorly* in the absence of his lucky glove.

The same principle is at stake when we analyze the market. What have you been told about the market that you believe is an iron truth? What correlations do you mistake for causation? Prior to 2008, millions of people believed that real estate was a safe investment that always increased in value. Many discovered in the most painful way that just because real estate *had* been going up, that didn't mean the correlation would remain static. Nor did it indicate a causal relationship. There's no guarantee that real estate will go up when the market goes up, or go up when the market goes down, or any other correlation.

These kinds of mistakes aren't solely the preserve of amateurs. I see financial professionals who believe that real estate trusts are a surefire hedge against volatility. It only takes a quick glance at history to disprove this hypothesis. Back in the 1980s, it was a fair summary. Now they move broadly in line with the market. That could easily change again.

As we discussed in chapter 2, one of the four assumptions of MPT is that correlations are static. In the real world, that's not the case. Correlations change all the time. The danger of this trap lies in the belief that it's safe to allocate assets in a way that would have represented solid investing several decades ago, even though correlations have shifted significantly since then.

The risk is that people assume correlations that were accurate years ago will remain accurate. They don't take the time to investigate current correlations or assess how the assets in their portfolio complement one another. When the market goes down, most or all of their assets are positively correlated with the market—moving in broadly the same direction. The consequence? They inevitably suffer big losses. When the 2008 financial collapse happened, how did portfolios set up in accordance with MPT perform? Most retail investors lost a substantial amount of money. It was a painful time for a lot of people.

When a market goes up, some stocks follow the market closely, others follow it loosely, while others may be negatively correlated. They drop in value while the market as a whole is increasing. Every single investment has a correlation—or covariance—number that stipulates how each individual stock fits into a portfolio. Ideally, a portfolio includes a few stocks that tend to be positively correlated with the market and a few that tend to be negatively correlated.

Smart investors, such as Ray Dalio, build portfolios including some stocks that are positively correlated with the market and others that are negatively correlated. They don't take a lot of positions; there's no diversification value in a dozen stocks that all broadly track the market. Instead, they select four or five positions, carefully chosen to hedge against risk.

Dalio's positions are correlated in a way that makes them complementary. He owns commodities, including some gold. He's invested in United States Treasury bonds. Around 30 percent of his portfolio is in stocks. He watches how these different assets perform relative to one another in good times and bad, and he diversifies in accordance with this relationship. If the relationship changes, he adapts his portfolio.

When markets collapse, for example, treasuries tend to do well. If the dollar starts to fade, gold goes up. Dalio knows this and invests to maximize his returns and minimize risk. This approach isn't sexy, but it works. Putting all this together is tricky and most investors overestimate their chances of doing it successfully. They simply don't have the tools to succeed. That's why expert help is so valuable.

STAY UP-TO-DATE WITH CORRELATIONS

Let's revisit our fictional jungle. You've arrived on its shores and all you can see is a dense, inhospitable environment. You can barely see fifty feet in front of you, and you have no idea what horrors await you if you tread unwarily or become lost.

Clearly, you need a guide. Who should you choose? Someone who tells you they traversed the jungle successfully twenty years ago, and who assures you that he still knows the way? Or someone who regularly treks among the trees to visit their cousin in another village, and who needs to understand the current state of the jungle to ensure he returns safely?

It's a no-brainer, isn't it? A jungle is a living organism. You wouldn't trust someone who hadn't been there in decades, because his knowledge wouldn't be current. The same principle applies to correlations. If you rely on correlations that were current in years gone by, you may find that you are exposed to excessive risk. If you assess how correlations shift, and adapt your strategy based on the most up-to-date information you can access, you will be in a much better position to build your portfolio.

The financial jungle is just as dangerous as a real jungle. It's incredibly easy to take wrong turns or fall foul of predators— even if the financial predators are more smartly dressed. Believing that correlations are static is simply adding another layer of wholly unnecessary danger. Don't do that to yourself. Get hold of the most recent map you can find, employ a guide who understands correlations, and design a portfolio to take you to your destination.

Some people treat the financial jungle like a casino, placing large bets in the hope of winning big. Unfortunately, those people are more likely to lose their shirt than celebrate major victories. In the next chapter, we'll discuss the gambler's mentality, manifested in the belief that greater risk equals greater reward.

Chapter Five

TRAP FIVE: THE MORE RISK I TAKE, THE GREATER MY POTENTIAL RETURN

When Ray came to me for a second opinion on his portfolio, he was in his early seventies. He presented the profile of a risk-taker, with a portfolio heavily invested in stocks. He had almost sixty individual positions, many of which he'd owned for a considerable time.

During our conversation, I asked him how comfortable he was, at his age, taking the substantial risks inherent in owning so many stocks. Ray was bullish in his response, insisting that the more risk he took, the greater his potential return.

It's an attitude I've encountered dozens of times, before and since. Many otherwise sane and sober investors insist that the path to financial success goes through the kind of risky bets that seem more at home in a casino.

In fact, Ray treated his portfolio as though managing it were a leisure activity. He didn't live off the proceeds of his investments and had no intention of using the money he accrued through the markets. Instead, he loved the thrill of winning and could afford the pain of losing money.

It's fortunate that he was in such a privileged position, because he ended up losing a substantial amount of money during the financial collapse of 2008. I lost touch with him after that, but it's safe to say that if he maintained the positions he took prior to the collapse, he will have taken several years just to recover, let alone to make more money.

One of the things I asked Ray when he was in my office was whether he knew how many small businesses fail within the first five years of opening. The answer is close to 80 percent. Anyone who decides to start a new business is taking a substantial risk. Sure, there's potential for solid—even spectacular—returns, but there's much more potential for failure.

The same is true for people who take a lot of risk in the stock market. Although they may end up winning big, it's more likely they'll take a hit. Ray could shrug and accept that scenario. He had enough money to last the rest of his life. For him, investing was a hobby. Most of us aren't so lucky.

The idea that high risk equals high potential return is perhaps the most dangerous trap in this book, because it tempts retail investors into taking risky positions they can ill afford. Supposedly reputable financial news sources push this narrative, lending it a credibility it doesn't deserve.

One of the key messages I want to give you is that it's vitally important to think for yourself, not simply to swallow the advice of others—including myself—whole. Before you take a position, do your research and investigate *why* you're doing so. Do you understand why it's a good idea, or are you simply doing what someone on television tells you to do?

As you grow older, this attitude becomes ever more important. It's one thing to learn a painful lesson when you're thirty-five with plenty of time to adjust your strategy accordingly. It's quite another to take a gut punch when you're seventy, and to lose money that you relied on to fund your retirement.

Far from taking more risk, it makes sense for most people to take *less* risk as they move into their sixties and seventies. By this stage of their lives, most affluent people are more interested in protecting and preserving their money than gambling on risky positions.

Gambling can be fun, as long as it remains a leisure activity rather than a compulsion. Ray illustrates the gambler's mentality; the belief that the next big score is just around the corner. He didn't need that money to survive, however, so he could afford to play fast and loose with his copious funds.

For anyone investing with a view to a comfortable retirement, the advice of Warren Buffett is apt. Buffett's first rule of investing is "Never lose money." The second? "See rule number one."

There may be times when taking more risk does indeed offer greater potential returns. The problem, however, is not the level of potential returns. It's the likelihood of gaining those returns. Most of the time, that likelihood is low, raising the question of whether taking so much risk is a good idea.

When people fail to plan early for future retirement, the idea that greater risk equals greater return is dangerously seductive. It looks like a way to compensate for starting late. Those who set up a retirement plan in their twenties or thirties can reduce overall risk to a low level. Across forty or fifty years, a smart investor can almost guarantee success. Staking a successful retirement on higher risk positions, later in life, is no substitute for a strategy based on gradual, low-risk accumulation.

UNDERSTAND YOUR RISKS

Mark Twain said, "It ain't what you know that gets you into trouble, it's what you know for sure that just ain't so." No one deliberately chooses to take excessive risk. The problem is that most people don't understand how much risk they're taking. They're lulled into a false sense of security by the financial media, by advisors, and by the dopamine hit they get when they open their statement and see that the value of their stocks has increased.

The wise way to read a statement is to recognize that gains on paper mean nothing until they're realized. It's all too easy when reading positive numbers month after month to conclude that the value of an asset will continue to appreciate indefinitely. Some people begin to extrapolate how much money they'll have if their stocks continue to rise at the same rate for another six months, a year, or even five years.

I've spoken to dozens of people who've fallen into that psychological trap. During a bull market, they read their statements and they're delighted by how quickly their investments are appreciating. They project into the future and start to dream of retiring a few months early.

Unfortunately, the market rarely works like that. Stocks can and do drop sharply. A healthy balance sheet can turn into a disaster area in the blink of an eye. Many people fall into the trap we described in the previous chapter: they confuse correlation with causation and come to believe that they can only succeed by taking a lot of risk. That's an erroneous—and dangerous—belief.

Let's use an example to illustrate how this can play out. A lot of financial advisors are comfortable advising clients to build a portfolio consisting of more stocks than bonds, in a ratio of 60/40, or even 70/30. They see this as normal and communicate as much to their clients. When the market turns, a portfolio consisting of so many stocks will suffer heavy losses, dealing a heavy financial and psychological blow to investors.

Most people trust their advisors and believe they're receiving good counsel—otherwise they wouldn't pay for it. They don't realize how much risk they're taking, and when they suffer major losses it comes as a total surprise. Like novices in a casino, they become intoxicated by the thrill of winning. Every month, they open their statement and count their gains. When they lose, they lose big, and it hurts.

We're psychologically biased to project forward into a future similar to today. But the stock market varies wildly from year to year, and even more from decade to decade. In 2018, the market was weak. As of September 2019, it's up around 20 percent on those lows. Anyone with a portfolio of 60 or 70 percent stocks is subject to huge fluctuations in the value of their investments, and a corresponding emotional roller coaster.

Smart investors think over time periods of ten, twenty, or thirty years. Instead of treating the stock market like a casino and looking to score a big win from a high-risk position, they plan their future carefully, understanding that gradually accruing gains will put them in a much better position than chalking up a track record of wins and losses.

The prospect of taking a major hit is scary. It should be. No one wants the sinking feeling that comes with watching a market crash and knowing they're exposed to significant losses. So let's take a look at what a balanced portfolio looks like.

A BALANCED PORTFOLIO

The bitterest irony of a portfolio consisting of 60 percent or more in stocks is that as it grows, it becomes more unstable.

Let's say that you choose to allocate 60 percent of your capital to stocks and 40 percent to bonds, already a fairly high-risk mix. Over a couple of years, your stock increases in value much more quickly than your bonds. What's the result? That stock now makes up a higher percentage of your portfolio. It may be as much as 70 or 75 percent of your total investments. Your bonds, meanwhile, are down to 25 or 30 percent of your portfolio.

Stocks are more volatile than bonds, so their increase in value means that the volatile component of your portfolio now makes up as much as three-quarters of your investments. The more your stocks go up, the higher your risk. When the market corrects, your losses will be eye-watering.

If you want to keep your risk constant, you need to readjust the balance of stocks and bonds as your investments grow. Periodically, perhaps once or twice a year, you must sell some and convert them into bonds or other secure investments. This reallocation will lock in your gains and protect you from incurring major losses.

When things are good, it's tempting to cross your fingers and hope that gains continue to accrue. Those who don't shift their gains into lower risk investments, however, see their portfolio become increasingly unstable, like a Jenga tower. The numbers keep going up, but the chances of the whole thing toppling become increasingly high.

What's most important is not how much you make, but rather how much you keep. Although numbers on a balance sheet *look* great, they're at constant risk of being snatched away. Many people think of investing like a yo-yo. They assume investments go up and down constantly, with no real way of controlling that movement. In fact, it's more like climbing a mountain. Preparing for retirement is a long-term goal that can and should take decades. Every time you take a step forward, secure that position so that you don't slide back down again. Only then are you ready to take the next step.

Investing Isn't a Yo-Yo

When a mountain climber gets halfway up a mountain, they may lose track of the summit. All they can do is take one step after the other, moving closer and closer to the top.

Eventually, the summit comes into view once again. Imagine what would happen if someone halfway up a mountain suddenly wanted to change course. That's exactly what's happening when a person constantly makes decisions based on their monthly statements.

Climbing the Financial Mountain

The pattern of investing followed by Ray is alarmingly common, but it's not universal. I've known people who understand the need to create a balanced portfolio and transfer the gains to lower-risk investments as they accrue.

Larry and June, for example, were a husband and wife I met through friends. They were sensible, conservative, and well-spoken, and when we talked about investing, they took a tack different from most people with whom I discuss finances on a casual basis. Instead of trying to impress me with their knowledge, they told me they didn't do a lot in stocks. Most of their money was in municipal bonds. During the financial collapse, their portfolio held steady. Bonds don't move a lot in price, so they didn't lose a substantial amount of money.

Larry's exposure to stocks was even lower than the percentage I describe above. He took 5 or 6 percent of his capital—which he called his "play account"—and dabbled in stocks. This was mainly for fun. If he won big, that was a bonus. If he lost big, it was nothing he couldn't afford. Larry and June understood their long-term goals and recognized that they didn't need to take a lot of risk to attain those goals. They represent a role model for investors who want to navigate the financial jungle safely.

One popular way to hedge against risk is to diversify—splitting assets among a range of different investments. The problem with this strategy is that many people misunderstand what diversification involves, as we'll discover in the following chapter.

Chapter Six

TRAP SIX: I'M DIVERSIFIED, I'LL BE OKAY

Tim was a real estate investor. He didn't invest in anything else, only in real estate. When he walked into my office, I was curious as to what motivated him. Why did he want to talk to someone like myself? What did he hope to gain from our conversation?

I didn't ask him outright, so I don't have a definitive answer to that question. My guess is that he saw the markets doing exceptionally well and he began to wonder whether he could secure stronger returns by broadening his focus. Perhaps, without admitting it to himself, he suspected that he was making some mistakes.

Tim sat down in my office and I asked him about his portfolio. He told me that he owned five different rental properties, from which he received a solid monthly income. In his mind, these properties represented a diversified portfolio, one that could withstand the slings and arrows of a capricious market.

Tim was confident, even a little cocky, until I decided to check whether he knew how to calculate his returns. I asked him whether he had any equity in his properties, and how he calculated the return on that equity.

Tim was using his rental income, minus his payments on the properties, to determine his returns. "I'm getting 5 to 6 percent," he said.

"No," I explained, "that's your cash flow." He had forgotten to factor in the capital tied up in each one of those properties.

I pressed him further. "You're getting 5 to 6 percent based on your monthly outgoings, but what's your return on the equity you've invested?" He looked at me, his brow creasing. I held up one hand, the tips of my thumb and forefinger meeting to form a circle. "Zero," I said. "It's zero."

Let's imagine that you own a property worth $200,000, in which you've invested $100,000. Your mortgage payments are $1,200 a month and you can charge $1,500 in rent. You're pulling in $300 a month, but you're not earning a penny on that $100,000.

Worse, you don't know exactly how much your property is worth. Sure, you know how much you *paid* for it, but the housing market fluctuates. Until you come to sell, you can't possibly know how much it will fetch. Stock market returns are advertised at the end of every day. Housing returns are uncertain until a property is sold.

Moreover, the equity in a property doesn't alter its overall value. Imagine a different scenario, in which you have just $50,000 in equity and a mortgage of $150,000. Is the value of the house different? Not by a cent.

When I explained all this, Tim became defensive and tried to justify his strategy. None of his bluster, however, changed the fact that all the equity he had plowed into his properties was dead money. In his efforts to build his net worth, it was contributing precisely nothing.

Tim was counting on the returns from his cash flow, not his equity. At the time, the housing market was strong, and he was reaping good returns, but like many people who are heavily invested in real estate, he had forgotten that it is a market like any other, a fact that was dramatically proven in 2008.

Tim assumed that he would always have people willing

to rent from him, guaranteeing him a steady income. In a buoyant housing market, he was probably right. In a financial crisis, he was dead wrong.

Following the 2008 financial collapse, millions of people lost their jobs. Many were left without the income to afford their monthly rent and responded by moving in with parents or other relatives. Others found themselves in straitened circumstances and downsized and rented out spare rooms to provide extra income, shrinking the overall rental market. In the worst cases, people lost their homes. For people in Tim's position, the pool of prospective renters diminished considerably.

Tim's strategy contained other holes. Property attracts taxes. Even people without a mortgage are vulnerable to repossession if they fall behind on their taxes. Who really owns the house when it can be taken away by the government to settle debts? In the state of Oregon, where I live, there is a state law mandating that property taxes must increase 3 percent annually. This is no small increase, particularly as it compounds year on year.

What about maintenance? Using a maintenance service can be costly. Tim told me he did all that himself. He may have saved money, but did he calculate the value of his time or the cost of materials? A standard calculation for landlords is that they need to put aside 1 percent of the total property price to make improvements, and another 1 percent for maintenance. These expenses eat into returns, whether landlords do the work themselves or employ someone else to do it.

I never spoke to Tim again, so I don't know for sure what happened to him. If he maintained his existing position, it's a near certainty that he took heavy losses when the housing market collapsed. For all my efforts to explain the errors in his thinking, he left my office convinced that he was diversified and that he'd be okay in the event of a market downturn.

The fundamental mistake Tim made, and which I still see many people making, was believing that his five different properties represented a diversified portfolio. Investing heavily in one market, even in numerous different assets, is *not* diversification. With all his investable capital tied up in the real estate market, Tim was heavily dependent on the success of that market. Its failure was his failure.

This is a confusing concept to many people. They absorb the idea that diversification is simply a matter of taking a number of different positions. When a downturn hits, their twenty different stocks, or five different rental properties, all suffer in exactly the same way. It turns out they're not diversified in any meaningful sense.

A truly diversified portfolio is one that's carefully set up to hedge against different types of market movement. If stocks rise, it will grow. If they fall, the damage will be limited. If there's a real estate crash, they have other types of investments.

COMMON DIVERSIFICATION MISTAKES

The most common diversification mistake is to take dozens of positions on the stock market, all of which broadly track the market's movement. This strategy works well as long as the market is going up. As soon as it starts to decline, those positions decline with it.

Another mistake, as we saw with Tim above, is to invest in several different properties. The properties may be different but they're all part of the same market. When that market tanks, the value of all those investments drop.

To tackle this problem, however, it may not be necessary to move into different types of investment. It may be possible to offset this concentration of assets by investing in real estate in other states or countries. Markets in different geographical locations may respond differently, offering protection from market crashes.

Investing in apartments, condos, and townhouses isn't diversification, unless there are good reasons to think they'll behave differently in response to a market downturn. Something similar is true of equities. It may be worth investing in domestic equities, foreign equities, emerging market equities, and international equities to spread the risk of loss.

Individual circumstances differ and diversified portfolios are crafted on a bespoke basis. The underlying point, however, is that diversification must include assets that will respond differently to specific market conditions, whatever those conditions may be.

At the other end of the diversification spectrum, many people tie all their money up in a certificate of deposit (CD). This is one of the lowest-risk investments available, backed by banks and federal insurers. The flipside is that CDs offer very low returns. They also take a very long time to mature.

Over the ten years to 2019, returns dropped as low as 1 or 2 percent. This lack of growth makes it difficult to offset interest taxes and inflation. Over time, CDs lose purchasing power, making them a poor solution to the diversification problem. Sure, they are unlikely to tank when the market undergoes a correction, but the gains they offer are insufficient to compensate for market losses. Therefore, they're not enough to hedge against losses from other types of investments.

Another common misstep of amateur investment is to

entrust half or a third of a portfolio to two or three differ-ent brokers. Each broker will invest uniquely, so that must constitute diversification, right?

The obvious problem with this approach is that there's no coordination among brokers. They may all be making the same mistakes. Even in the best-case scenario, their invest-ments won't represent a coherent strategy. Would you hire three different contractors to build your home, assigning one the master bedroom, one the kitchen, and one the bathroom? Obviously not. It would be chaos.

If you've got three brokers managing a third each of your portfolio, you're in a similar situation. Do the brokers care that your portfolio is a mess? Not really. They get paid what-ever happens. They probably won't ever speak to each other. You're the one who will end up with a house—or in this case a portfolio—reminiscent of Frankenstein's monster.

HOW TO DIVERSIFY PROPERLY

We've discussed how *not* to diversify. The good news is that it's perfectly possible to diversify effectively. There are plenty of solid opportunities in the investment world. The key to taking advantage of them is knowing where you want to go and which ones will take you there.

Imagine standing at a bus stop. A bus pulls up in front of

you. How do you decide whether to get on? You know where you want to go and determine whether the bus will take you there. But what if you don't know where you're going? In that case, you don't know whether to get on the bus!

Now, what happens if you can't afford the fare? The doors of the bus will close, and it will move on to its destination without you. To invest wisely, you need to know where you're going and be prepared to take advantage of opportunities that arise.

Sometimes people come to me saying that they've tried several different investment strategies without success. It turns out they've been doing the equivalent of riding the bus aimlessly, not knowing their destination but hoping that it will get them there.

Putting the example in this context makes it sound ridiculous, but taking such a careless attitude to vital financial decisions is even more ridiculous. When I mentor young people, I talk to them about the importance of having five-year and ten-year plans. I want them to know where they're going. Only then can they figure out how to get there.

What does diversification look like in practice? A typical client of mine wants to spread their risk across a range of sectors. In addition to a diverse portfolio of stocks, they may own a business and some real estate. They keep cash and capital in distinct markets with a percentage of their investments in lower-risk areas such as bonds.

Should we encounter a recession, their business may suffer somewhat. On the other hand, the value of their real estate may remain strong. Some of their stocks will drop in value, whereas others—if they're properly correlated—will hold steady or even grow.

In summary, they understand their goals and they're well placed to withstand the vagaries of the market. They have a solid financial plan and they're not distracted by short-term fluctuations. Of course, they adapt if necessary, but when they do this, it's in service of their larger goals, not as a knee-jerk reaction to unfavorable market conditions.

David Swensen exemplifies this approach. He maintains a diverse portfolio, with 30 percent or less of the capital he manages in domestic equities, 15 percent in foreign equities or stocks, and 10 percent in emerging market stocks. In addition, he has 15 percent in inflationary-protected bonds, 15 percent in United States Treasuries, and 15 percent in real estate investment trusts—a way to receive dividends from owning property without covering the costs of maintenance. Over the course of twenty years, Swensen has delivered average returns of 13.9 percent a year for Yale University.

FOUR CRITERIA FOR EVALUATING INVESTMENTS

Different types of investments offer varying benefits. When you're evaluating an investment, there are four criteria to take into account: **cost, liquidity, safety**, and **rate of return**.

Let's consider real estate. Are houses costly? Absolutely. For many people, a house is the largest purchase they will ever make. Do houses represent liquid assets? No. Typically, it's difficult or impossible to sell a house within a week or two. Anyone who does this will likely receive much less than market value. How about safety? The housing crash notwithstanding, real estate usually offers a reliable income. Rate of return? In the United States, the national average is 4 percent growth in house prices per year.

Other assets represent different possibilities and problems. Stocks, for example, may deliver a higher rate of return than real estate. They're more liquid. They're less costly, although it's still fairly costly to invest at a level high enough to provide strong returns. The downside, of course, is that stocks are far more risky than real estate. They can drop in value with no warning.

The key to diversification is understanding how your investments rate in terms of the four criteria described above. If they're all similar, you're probably not diversified.

All your assets need to be working together to grow your net worth. The greater your net worth, the sooner you can retire and the more comfortable your retirement will be. Take the time to plan where you want to go and develop a strategy that will get you there.

Diversifying effectively is perfectly achievable. A business entrepreneur I will call Don runs a specialty manufacturing business that provided him with a substantial income. He owns properties in different states and maintains a well-diversified stock portfolio, so he's not too reliant on any one particular investment.

That's an ideal situation. Not everyone can own a multimillion-dollar business, but everyone can plan for their retirement, consider the relative strengths and weaknesses of different investments, and balance them so that they complement one another. Choose your investments wisely, be disciplined, and allow compounding to work its magic. The sooner you start planning for your financial future, the faster you'll see results.

In the final chapter of this book, we'll examine the huge toll taken by fees, a toll of which most investors are totally unaware.

Chapter Seven

TRAP SEVEN: FEES AREN'T A BIG DEAL

The late 1990s was a phenomenal time to be invested in tech stocks, with gains of up to five hundred points per day.

Naturally, thousands of investors were attracted to the stocks, excited by the potential gains. At times, it seemed as though it was impossible to go wrong. Many of the clients I saw during that time were intoxicated by how much money they were making. They were on a constant adrenalin rush as they watched their investments increase in value. The kind of hysteria I saw during those times has always been an indication that the situation is unsustainable, and of course the tech bubble burst a few years later. At the time, however, it was in full swing.

One of the people I met at that time was a gentleman named David. David wasn't a client. He was interested in investigating what it would be like to work with an advisor. Like many people who think they're better off investing on their own, David had a swagger about him. He was making a lot of money from tech mutual funds and he doubted that I could improve his portfolio.

I saw people like David a lot. I also knew that when fees were subtracted from their dividends they were making far less than they thought. Some funds claimed that they provided year-on-year returns touching 100 percent. In reality, that wasn't the case.

David challenged me, saying, "Why do I want to work with somebody like you when I can get 100 percent return on my own?"

I took up the challenge and answered, "Prove to me that your investment dollar grew by 100 percent and I'll buy you lunch anywhere in town, no strings attached." I never bought him lunch.

Why not? For the average investor, fees and expenses take a huge amount of money off the table. Too many people see fees as an incidental expense, when in fact they're crucial. David didn't even know how to calculate his true returns.

Over the course of a year, a 100 percent return means a doubling of each investment dollar. In David's case, the 100 percent figure represented a gross return, prior to applying fees and expenses. The net figure was significantly lower. When I went through the figures and showed David how much he was actually paying in fees, he was gobsmacked.

His earnings were good, but the fees ate up a huge proportion of those earnings. Investing in mutual funds meant that his positions changed frequently, meaning that he incurred a lot of trading expenses. By the time we'd calculated those trading expenses, David's cocky smile had turned to a frown.

I used Morningstar, a third-party independent research firm, to show David that he was paying well over 2 percent in trading costs. He was also paying 12b-1 fees, which are distribution fees, along with administrative and management fees. In total, he was paying almost 6 percent in fees per year, eating significantly into his profits.

HOW TO UNDERSTAND FEES

The Securities and Exchange Commission (SEC) does not require mutual funds to disclose trading costs to the investor. On April 4, 2011, Forbes published an article detailing types of funds and their associated fees.[4] The article

---

4   Ty A. Bernicke, "The Real Cost of Owning a Mutual Fund," *Forbes*, April 4, 2011.

revealed that the average stock mutual fund charged a 4.1 percent annual fee on a taxable account, or 3.7 percent on a nontaxable account.

The most common fees are called an expense ratio. Expense ratios typically cover costs such as auditing, marketing, and management fees. In most cases, they're calculated daily and can run from 1.25 to 1.5 percent of the average stock mutual fund. The average trading cost for a stock mutual fund comes in at about 1.44 percent.

Add that 1.25 percent and 1.44 percent together, then add on other fees such as 12b-1 fees. Mutual fund markets don't employ salespeople to pitch their funds. Instead, they engage wholesalers who go to Wall Street firms and try to convince the firms to purchase their family of funds. That advocacy costs money, which is then passed along to the investor.

Failing to fully and carefully investigate fees is one of the most common mistakes people make when selecting their investments. The problem is compounded by the ignorance of many brokers, who are equally fuzzy on the details of fees.

Magazines and television commercials present an ideal world in which investors can hire a mutual fund manager and trust that their money is in good hands. A sloppy attitude to fees, however, can cost those people as much as 30 or 40 percent of their investment returns.

The key fact to understand is that fees compound, just as returns do. What seems like a small percentage can, over time, become a huge problem. To illustrate how much difference fees can make, let's compare three hypothetical investors, Shirley, Barbara, and Jane. They're all the same age and, when they reach thirty-five, each one invests $100,000 in a mutual fund that delivers consistent annual returns of 7 percent. The only difference in their investments is how much they pay in fees. Shirley pays 3 percent, Barbara 2 percent, and Jane 1 percent.

Thirty years after their original investments, Shirley, Barbara, and Jane cash in their mutual funds. Shirley's $100,000, growing at 7 percent minus 3 percent in annual fees, has grown to $324,340. Barbara's $100,000, at the same rate of return minus 2 percent in annual fees, is now worth $432,194. Jane's $100,000, with her 1 percent fees, is up to $574,349.

All three women invested the same amount of money and achieved the same returns, yet over thirty years fees cost Shirley $250,000 more than Jane.

Fees can lead to other nightmare scenarios. A man named Todd came to see me with his wife. Todd was looking for a second opinion on his holdings to determine whether he was on track for retirement. He had recently sold his business, a pharmacy he had owned for years, and invested the proceeds.

Todd laid out all of his holdings for me, and I noticed that one of them was a variable annuity. I asked him to explain how it worked. He replied, "The last installment, the balloon payment on selling my business, was $1.2 million. I was referred to a gentleman who suggested that I put that $1.2 million into a variable annuity, which I did. He told me that by doing so, I was guaranteed $100,000 a year for life."

I asked Todd how much he was paying in fees and he said 1.2 percent. He had the prospectus for his annuity with him and he gave me permission to review it, which I did. As I looked through it, I circled the fees, including an income rider. When I showed him in black and white what he was actually paying, the number was closer to 4.5 percent.

Even after I explained that, Todd was sanguine. He figured that if his variable annuity guaranteed him $100,000 a year for the rest of his life, it must be pretty good. He had a shock coming.

By the time Todd sought out my advice, a few years after he signed his contract, his account had grown to almost $2 million. As his money grew, so did his fees. When I saw him, his $100,000 a year was costing him $80,000 dollars per year in fees. As his money continued to grow, his fees grew with it. A couple of years later, he was paying more than $100,000 per year in fees.

Until I laid it out for him, Todd had no idea how much he paid in fees. Worse, he had signed a nine-year contract which imposed stiff penalties, known as surrender fees, if he canceled. Generally, surrender fees run to 9 percent of the current value of the holdings in the first and second years, then 8, 7, 6, 5, 4, all the way down to 2 percent for canceling in the final year remaining. This structure locks investors in, making it more costly to cancel the agreement than continue with it.

Although Todd was paying excessive fees, I couldn't recommend that he cancel his agreement. Had he done so the costs would have become even greater. I don't know how much his portfolio grew, but if it reached $2.5 million, Todd would have paid $112,500 annually in fees for his guaranteed $100,000.

The harsh and painful lesson he learned was that the annuity company with which he invested was not his friend. The business model was set up for the company to make money off clients. The more Todd's investment grew, the more money he made for the annuity company.

TAKE CONTROL OF FEES

In *Money: Master the Game*, Tony Robbins explains how financial fees usually work.

"Here's the game and this is how it goes. Someone wants you to put up 100 percent of the capital and take 100 percent of the risk. If it makes money, he wants 60 percent or more of the upside to come to him in fees. Oh, and by the way, if it loses money, you lose and he still gets paid."[5]

The question is, do you want to play that game? If you have money invested in mutual funds, you've already agreed to those terms.

Understanding fees is a crucial element of investing. Unfortunately, the average investor doesn't understand the fees they will be charged. In some cases, even the people they hire to look after their interests don't understand the fees their firm charges.

According to Morningstar, Forbes, and other independent sources, 85 to 90 percent of mutual funds fail even to match their benchmark, let alone outperform it. The average investor pays a substantial amount of money for underperformance in the marketplace. This is a tragedy that eats away at the prosperity of thousands of people, perhaps millions. Unsurprisingly, there is little pressure from within the industry for the financial media to disclose to people how much they're paying.

---

5   Tony Robbins, *Money: Master the Game: 7 Simple Steps to Financial Freedom* (New York: Simon & Schuster, 2014), 84.

If you want to take control of your fees, I can only suggest that you engage a registered investment advisor. We have a fiduciary responsibility to always put our clients' best interests ahead of our own, meaning that we are legally bound by that responsibility.

Most financial advisors operate to a far lower standard, known as suitability. The only criteria they need to meet is to ascertain whether the products they sell meet the client's stated objectives.

Unlike the arcane and confusing fee structure detailed above, my firm charges a yearly management fee. On average, this breaks down to 1 percent of assets under management, paid in four quarterly installments. There are no extra fees, no transaction costs, and no other hidden charges. This is the type of fee structure you should look for from a reputable registered investment advisor.

CONCLUSION

As we discussed, in chapter 2, the 2018 DALBAR report clearly shows that do-it-yourself investors receive substantially lower returns than those who work with a competent advisor. Over the course of ten years, the average investor receives a return of 4.8 percent through working with an advisor. By contrast, the same investor navigating the investment jungle solo receives a return of just 2.52 percent.

Solo investors tend to see the world and the markets through different lenses, leading to numerous categorical errors. For example, they make rash judgments, time their moves poorly, and succumb to panic caused by a lack of information and experience. Together, these mistakes equate to poor performance.

Industry expert, Bob Arnott, who founded Research Affiliates, spent two decades studying the top two hundred actively managed mutual funds with at least $100 million under management. The results he uncovered are stunning.

Between 1994 and 1998, only eight of two hundred fund managers outperformed the Vanguard 500 Index. That's a mere 4 percent.[6] There are roughly 7,900 mutual funds in existence and 4,900 individual stocks. All of those mutual funds claim that they can help you to beat the market. Over an extended period of time, however, 96 percent of them are mistaken.

This is no surprise. When we're stressed or anxious, we feel a lot of pressure to act. In situations where we feel isolated, lacking any feedback to moderate our fears, we may well reach for a knee-jerk solution. There are four common tendencies that lead inexperienced investors down blind alleys:

1. **Optimism.** Many people enter the financial markets with an unrealistic assessment of the dangers. They overestimate how likely it is that good things will happen to them and underestimate how likely they are to fall foul of the many traps and predators in the financial jungle.
2. **Media response.** The media presents a sensationalized view of the markets. People who rely on financial news to make investing decisions are liable to be caught in

---

6   Bob Arnott, Fundamental Index newsletter, March 2009.

a whirlwind, constantly convinced that they need to change their plans to take advantage of movements in the market. This is especially true in volatile markets, which tend to spark enthusiasm and panic in equal measure.

3. **Herd mentality.** When we don't know what to do, we tend to copy the behavior of others. This is a common factor in the markets. During prolonged down periods, when many investors are selling their assets, it's tempting for investors to assume that others have inside information and to also sell. Individual investors are likely to be influenced by the overall mood of a market, taking undue risk in one area while avoiding sensible risk in another.

4. **Regret.** Retail investors tend to look upon errors of commission more seriously than errors of omission. They may become distressed by losses they have already incurred, allowing them to wield a disproportionate influence on future investing behavior.

Far too many people fall into the traps described in this book, suffering financial damage and misery as a result. The most painful aspect of these losses is that with better planning and advice they could have been avoided.

It's important to understand that the world of finances really is comparable to a jungle. It's wild, often unregulated, and packed with hazards for the unwary traveler. Like a jungle, however, it's possible to survive and thrive with good preparation and support.

Too many amateur investors rely on financial television for that support. It's not a wise choice. Financial television trades on drama. In a volatile environment, the last thing investors need is more anxiety and adrenalin. You wouldn't take someone into the jungle with you who screamed, "Oh my God! A snake!" whenever they saw a tree vine. For the same reason, you shouldn't rely on financial television to give you a levelheaded picture of the financial landscape.

CHOOSING A GUIDE TO THE FINANCIAL JUNGLE

If you're not familiar with the terrain, you'll want to hire a guide to help you plot a path through the financial jungle. The first thing to consider is that there are different types of advisors.

A registered investment advisor has a fiduciary duty to you. A broker doesn't. If you're not certain that you're working with a registered investment advisor, check. Understand how your advisor is incentivized. Whose side are they really on?[7]

---

7   For a clever animation from Bespoke Wealth Management depicting the distinctions between a broker and a registered investment advisor, visit https://www.youtube.com/watch?v=PQQzzLauAdA.

Registered investment advisors charge a flat fee for advice. They may charge by the hour or by percentage of assets under management. Brokers usually receive a flat fee in addition to commission, meaning they get paid whenever clients move money.

Perhaps you've heard of Dodd-Frank, a bill named after the two congressional members who proposed it. Dodd-Frank is the bill that enshrines the distinction between a fiduciary responsibility and the role of a standard broker.

Incredibly, there was some controversy over the question of whether putting the client's best interest first is a good thing to do. Mutual fund companies and asset managers make millions of dollars from investors. It's in their interests to limit discussion of the fiduciary standard. You might imagine that every advisor puts their clients' interests first. Unfortunately, you'd be wrong.

My specific niche is wealth management, working with clients who have a million dollars or more in investible assets. Most of my clients own small-to-medium-sized enterprises (SMEs). These people seek me out for a combination of returns and wealth protection. I assist them in growing their wealth sustainably, minimizing their taxes, and making charitable donations.

Every person is unique and everyone I work with has their

own specific goals. As a general rule, however, most are concerned with their retirement and their legacy. They want to know that every aspect of their financial life is handled.

The basis of my wealth management formula is simple, although applying it is complex and subtle. It looks like this:

Wealth Management (WM) = Investment Consulting (IC) + Advanced Planning (AP) + Relationship Management (RM)

Investment consulting combines a broad range of investment elements, such as assessing portfolio performance, evaluating risk, and allocating assets. This area also covers investigating fees and other expenses, minimizing taxation, and the creation of an investment policy statement.

The Wealth Management Formula

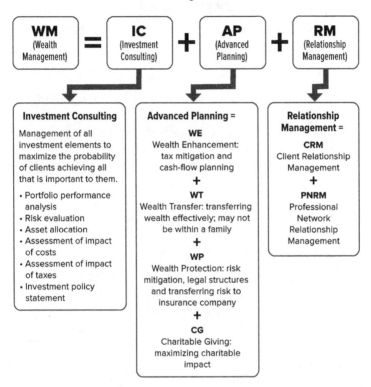

The Wealth Management Formula (Credit: CEG Advantage)

Advanced planning consists of wealth enhancement, which covers tax mitigation, cash flow planning, and wealth transfer plus wealth protection, consisting of risk mitigation, legal structure, and transferring risk to insurance companies, along with charitable giving.

Relationship management breaks down into two sections. The first is client relationship management, which involves meeting regularly with a client to discover and understand their goals. The second is professional network relationship, which can involve connecting clients with highly knowledgeable attorneys and certified public accountants (CPAs) who have expertise in areas I don't. Virtual Family Office (VFO) incorporates all aspects of wealth management.

The Wealth Management Hierarchy (Credit: CEG Advantage)

WHAT NEXT?

Thanks for taking this guided tour through the investment jungle! I hope you've found the information in this book valuable and that you feel a little more ready to tackle the traps that abound.

To continue your explorations, please visit www.navigatetheinvestmentjungle.com. There you can fill out a free questionnaire and register for webcasts where we'll explore the subjects raised in this book in greater depth.

If you'd like to explore working directly with me, please email me at dstone@seacrestwm.com, or call toll-free at 866-240-0617. The first step for all potential new clients is a complimentary forty-five-minute evaluation, in which we will dive into your financial life, assessing your values, goals, relationships, assets, and any other relevant factors.

Finally, if you'd like me to come and speak to your business, school, club, or any other organization, please use the same email address and phone number to get in touch. I love sharing stories of my years in the jungle and sharing advice with those who want to know.

Whatever steps you take, please be careful out there. The investment jungle is a dangerous and unpredictable place, although it can also be highly rewarding. Here's to your financial success!

ABOUT THE AUTHOR

DOUGLAS STONE is a wealth advisor with SeaCrest Wealth Management, who brings twenty-three years of experience to his work with affluent households. Douglas began questioning his industry's approach seven years into his career, and in 2009, he left the major wirehouse where he worked to become an independent advisor.

For six years, he discussed his self-taught, holistic approach to wealth management on *Real Money with Doug Stone*, a radio program on KMED 1440 AM in Medford, Oregon. Today, Doug shares his knowledge and expertise through workshops, seminars, and speaking engagements.

CPSIA information can be obtained
at www.ICGtesting.com
Printed in the USA
LVHW050811060620
657560LV00003B/853